Vol.1
Ed.2

Gothic Girls

grayscale coloring book

by

Tabz Jones

FIRST EDITION 2016

TABZ JONES
PO BOX 2137
ALMA, AR. 72921
WWW.GOTHICTOGGS.NET

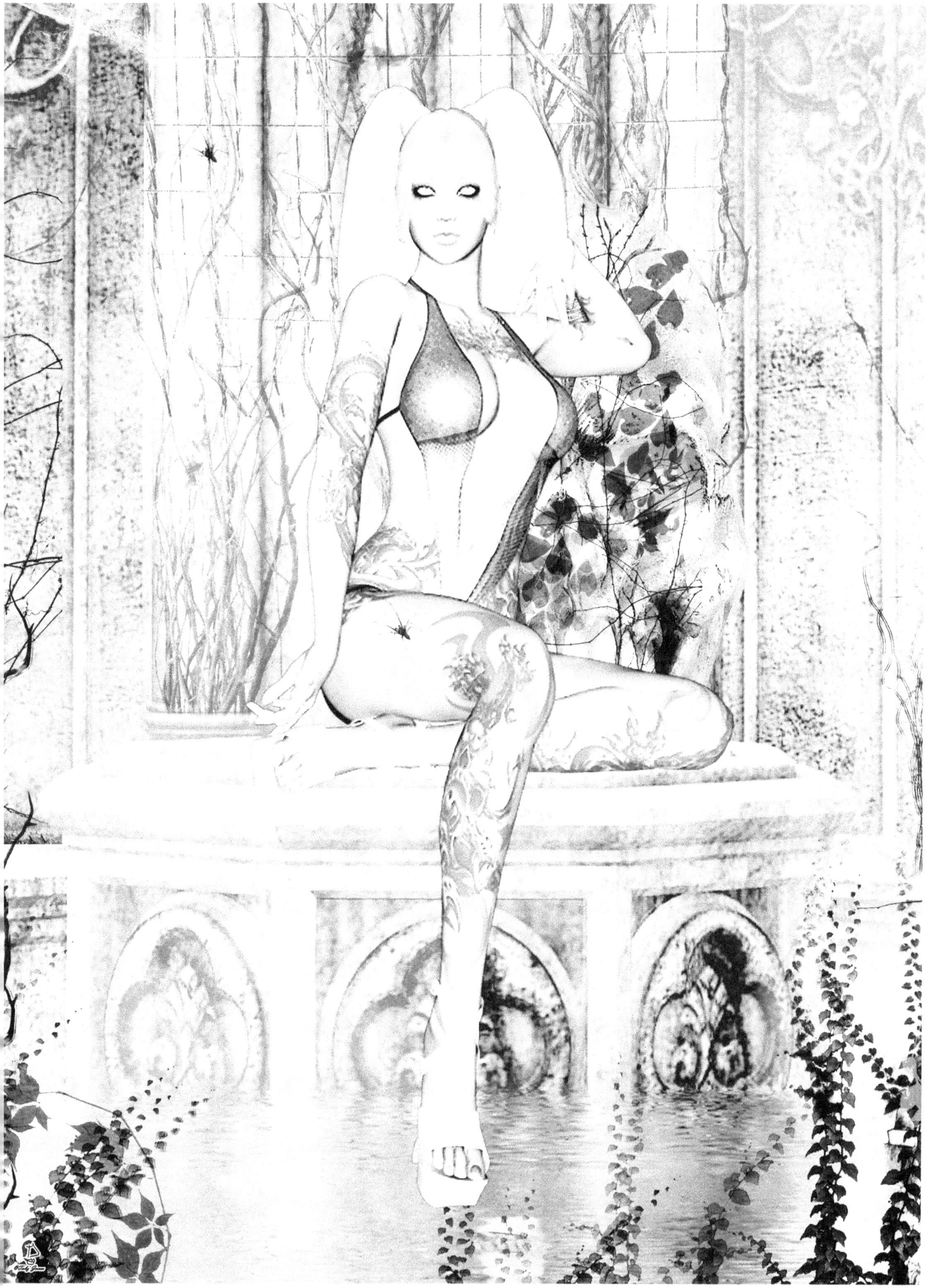

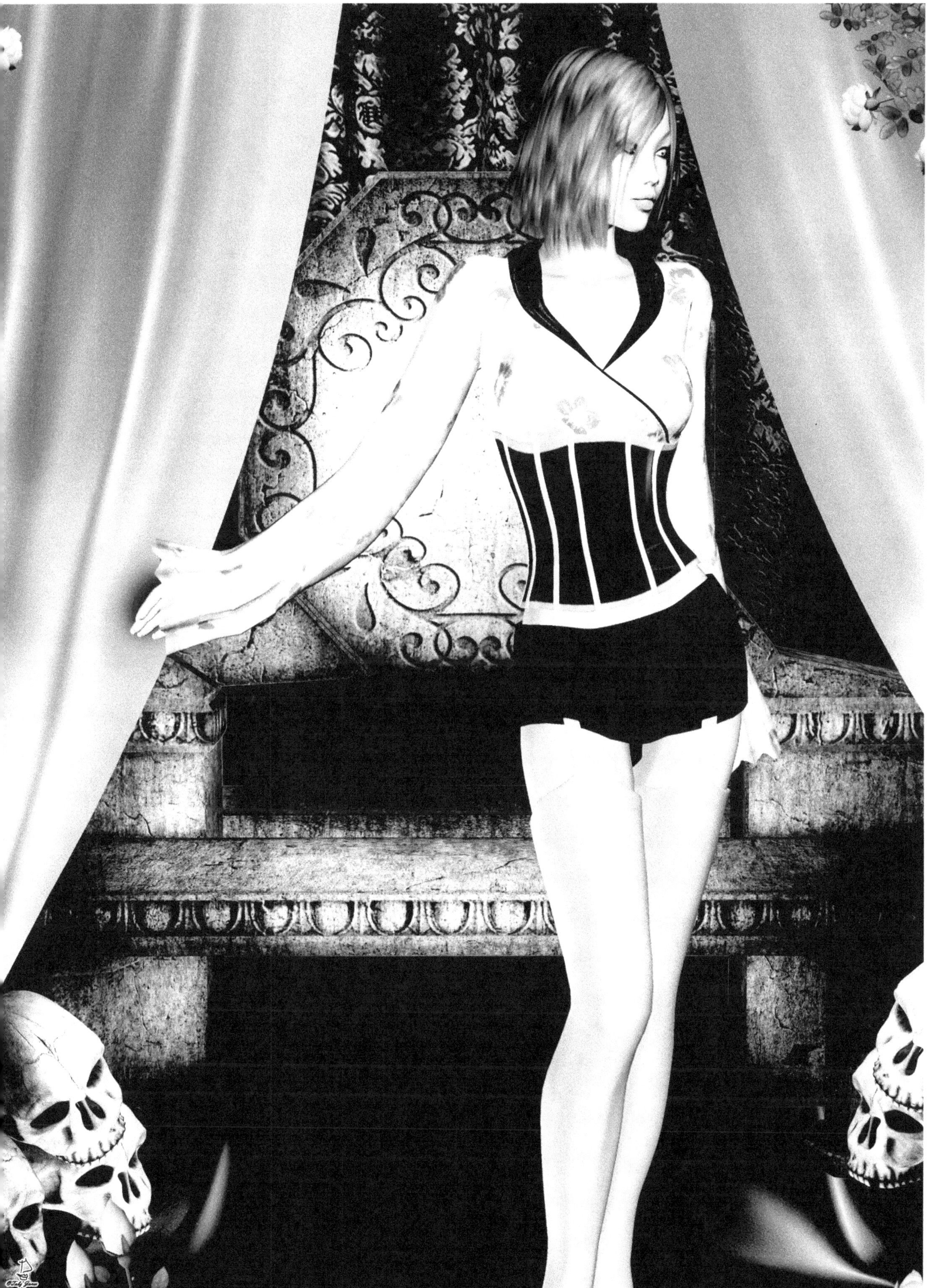

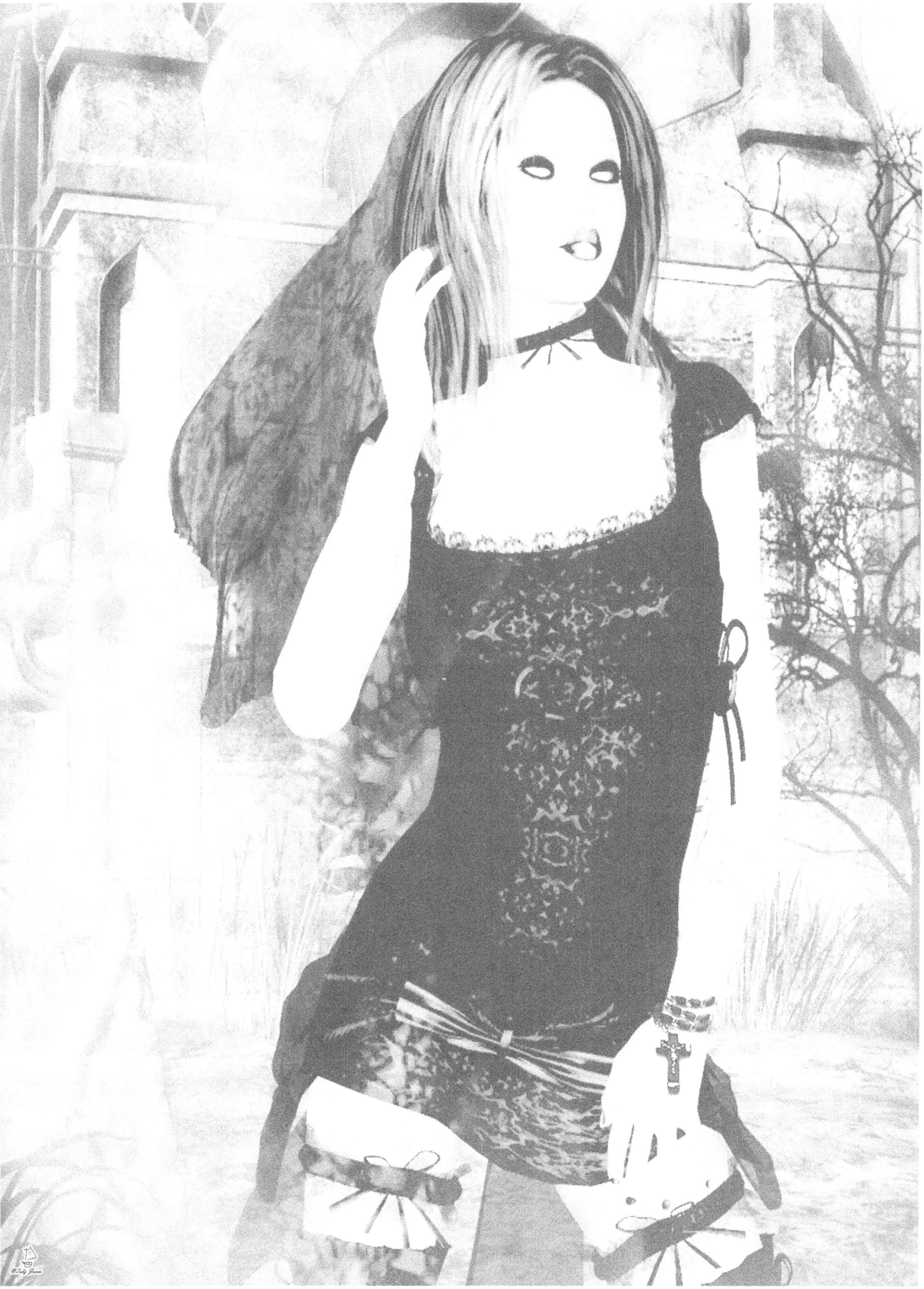

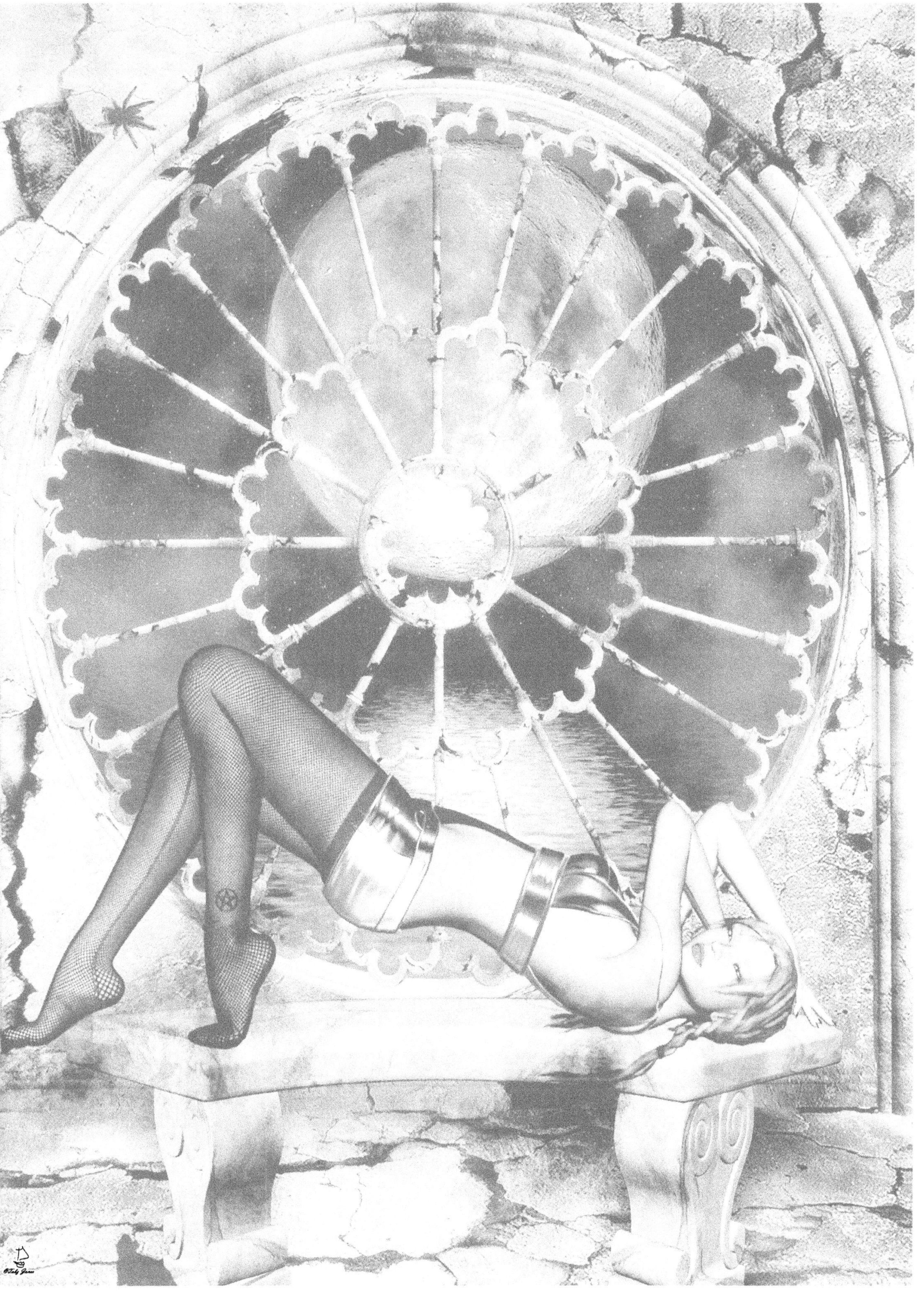

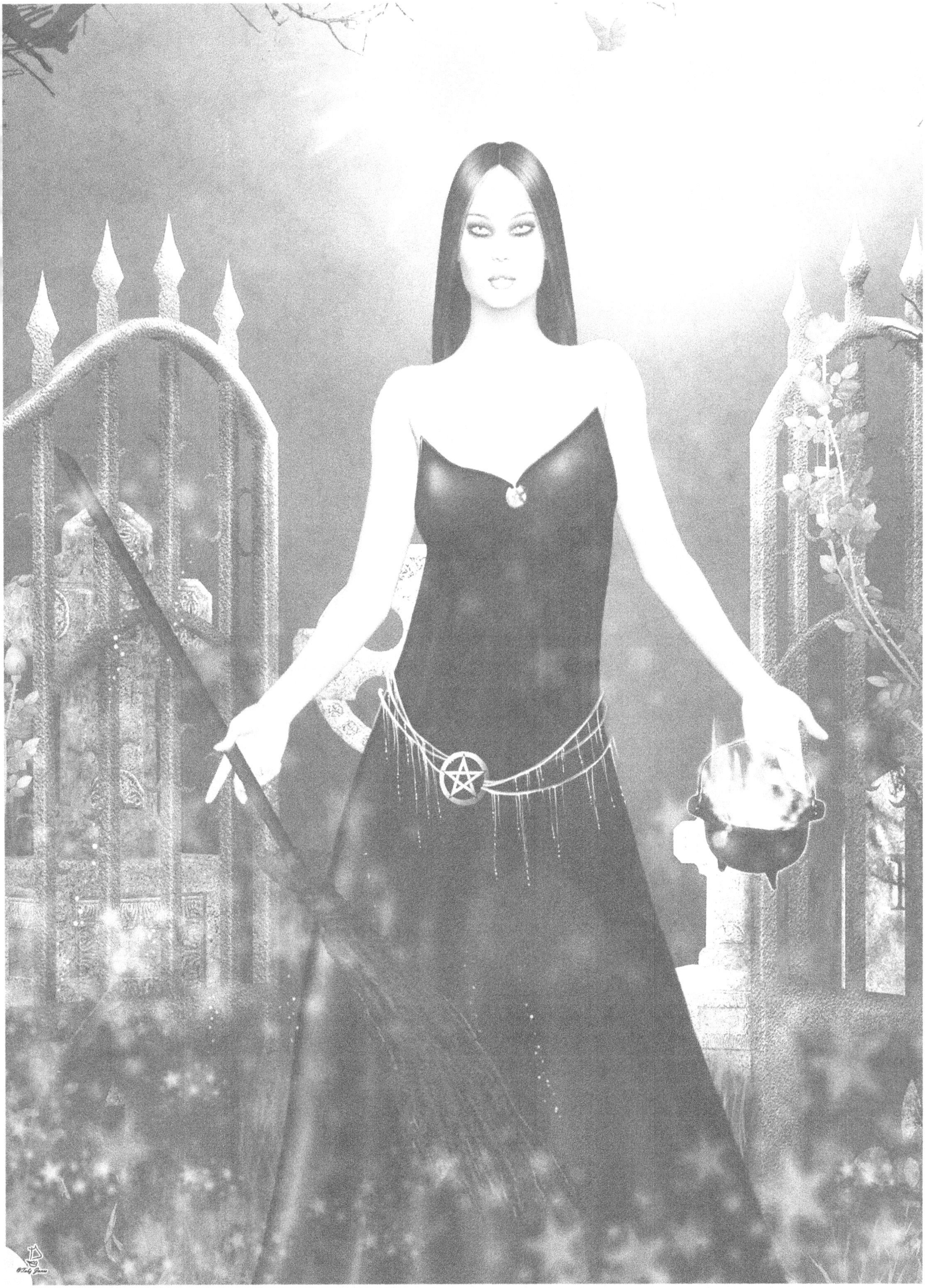

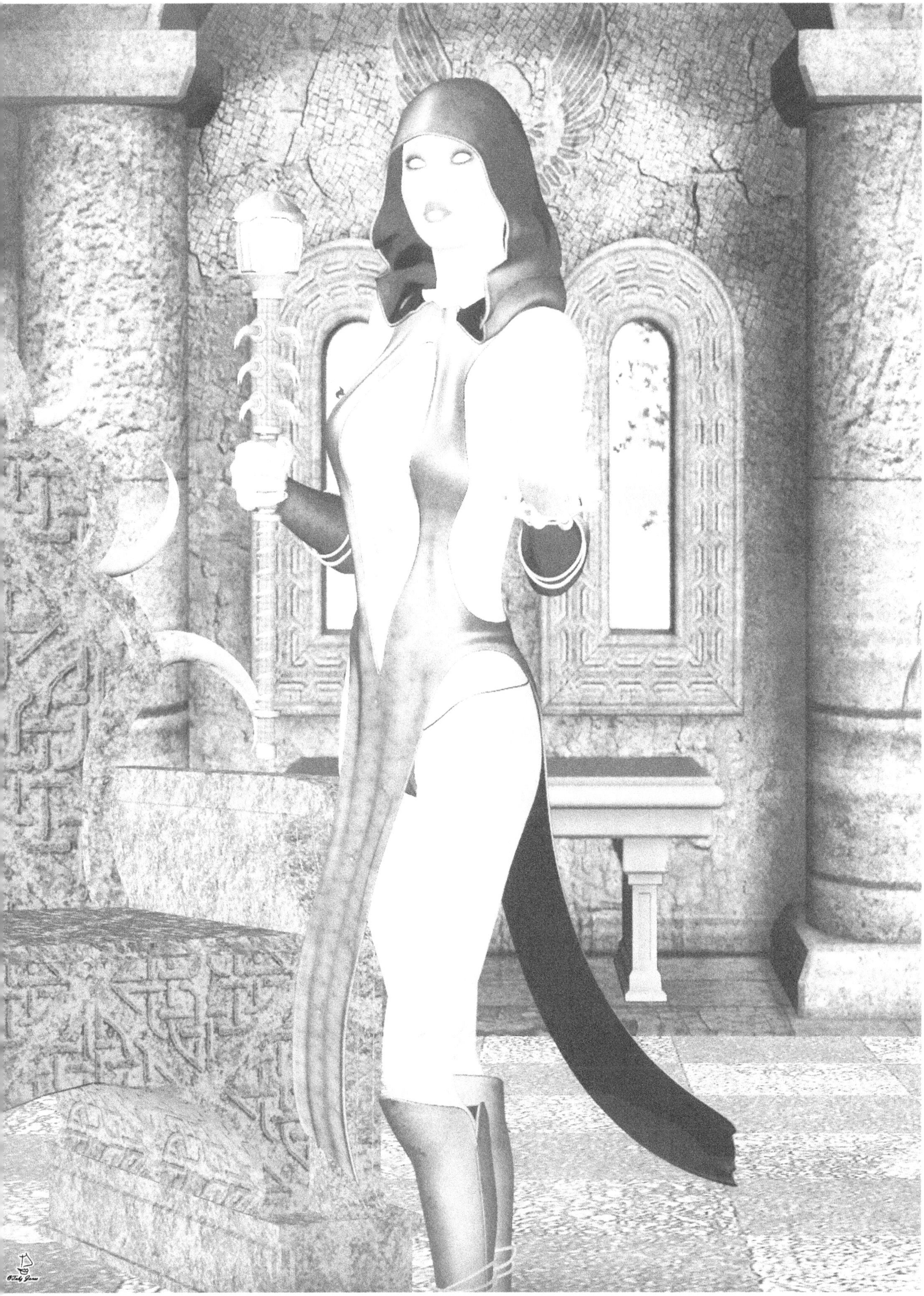

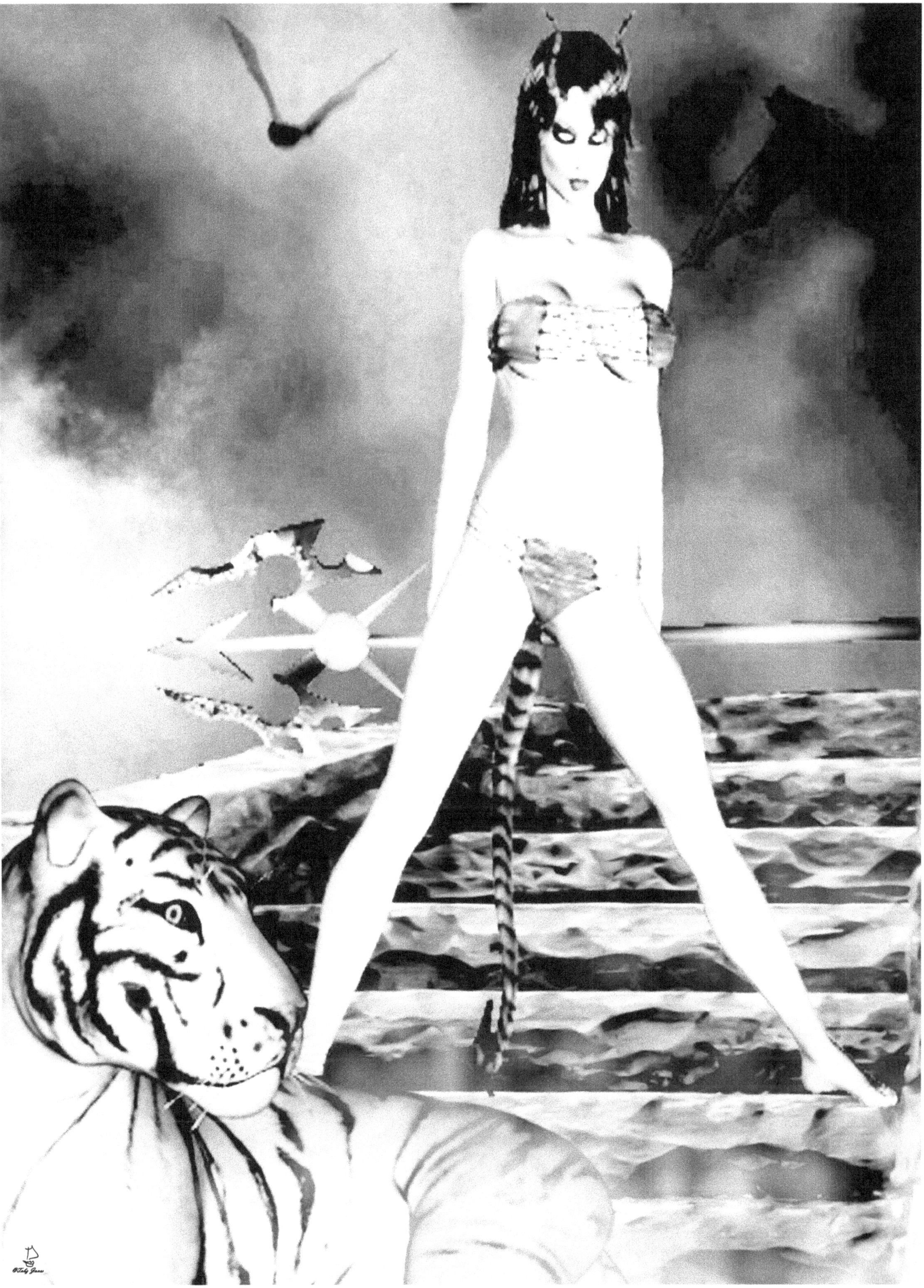

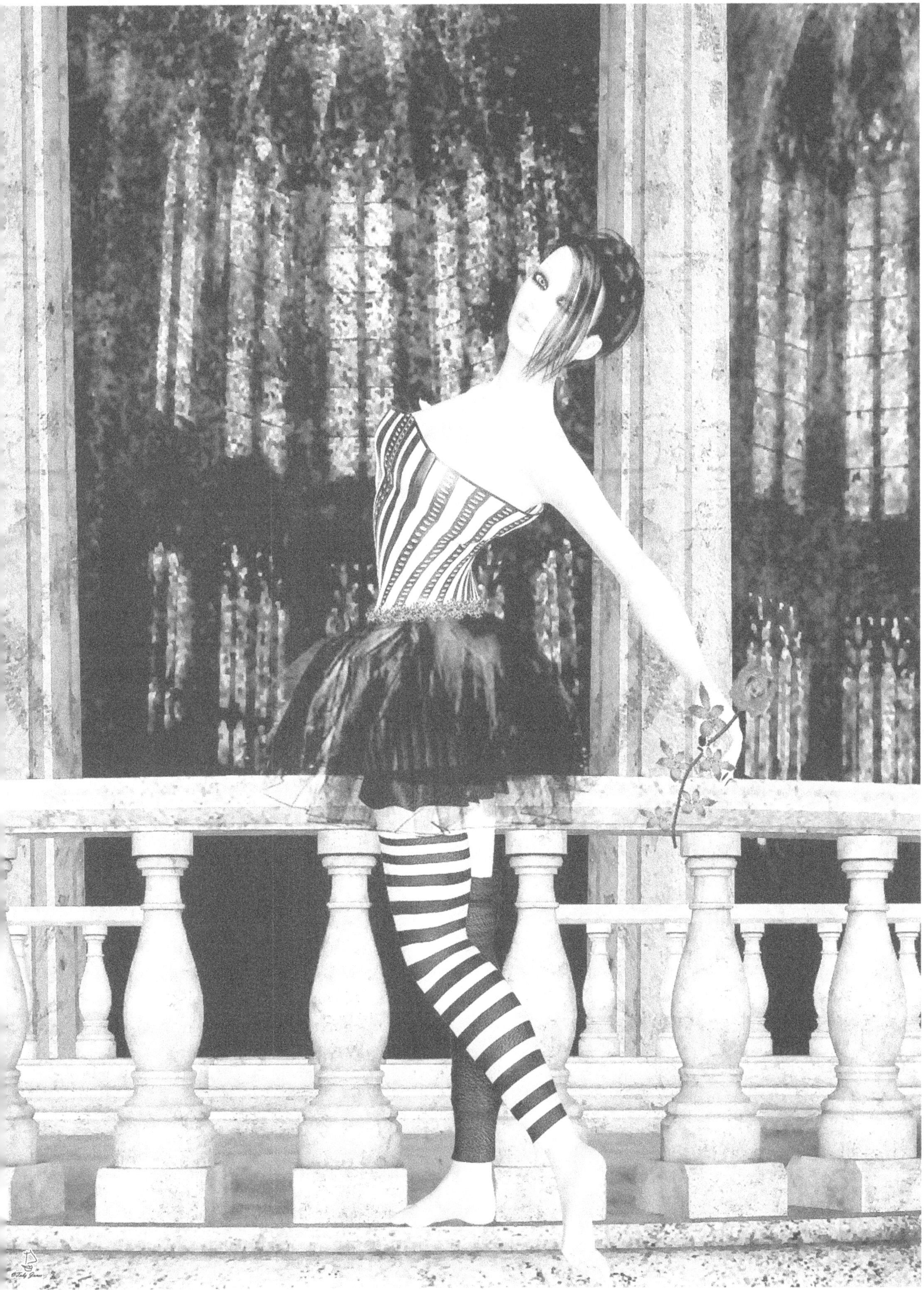

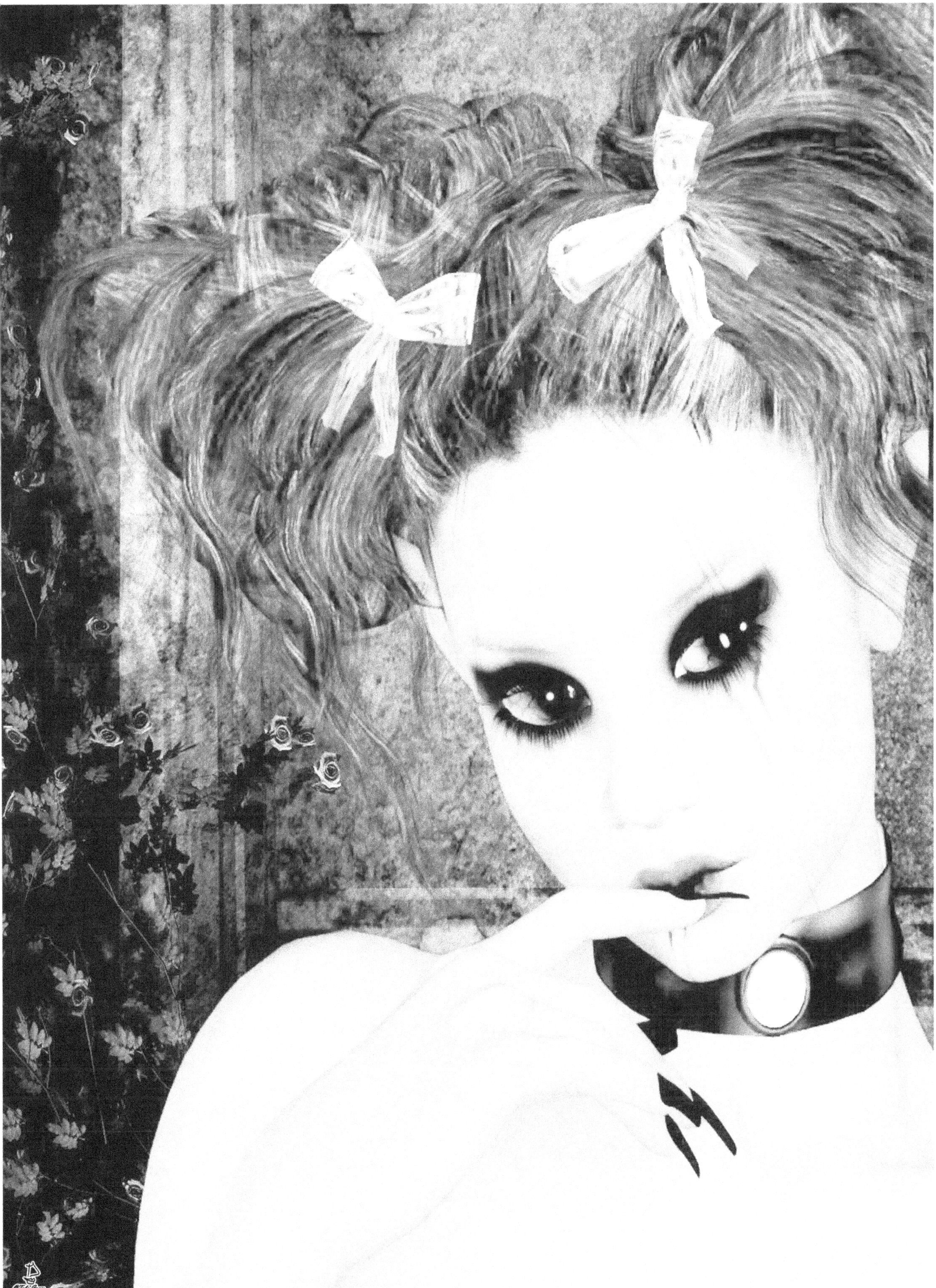

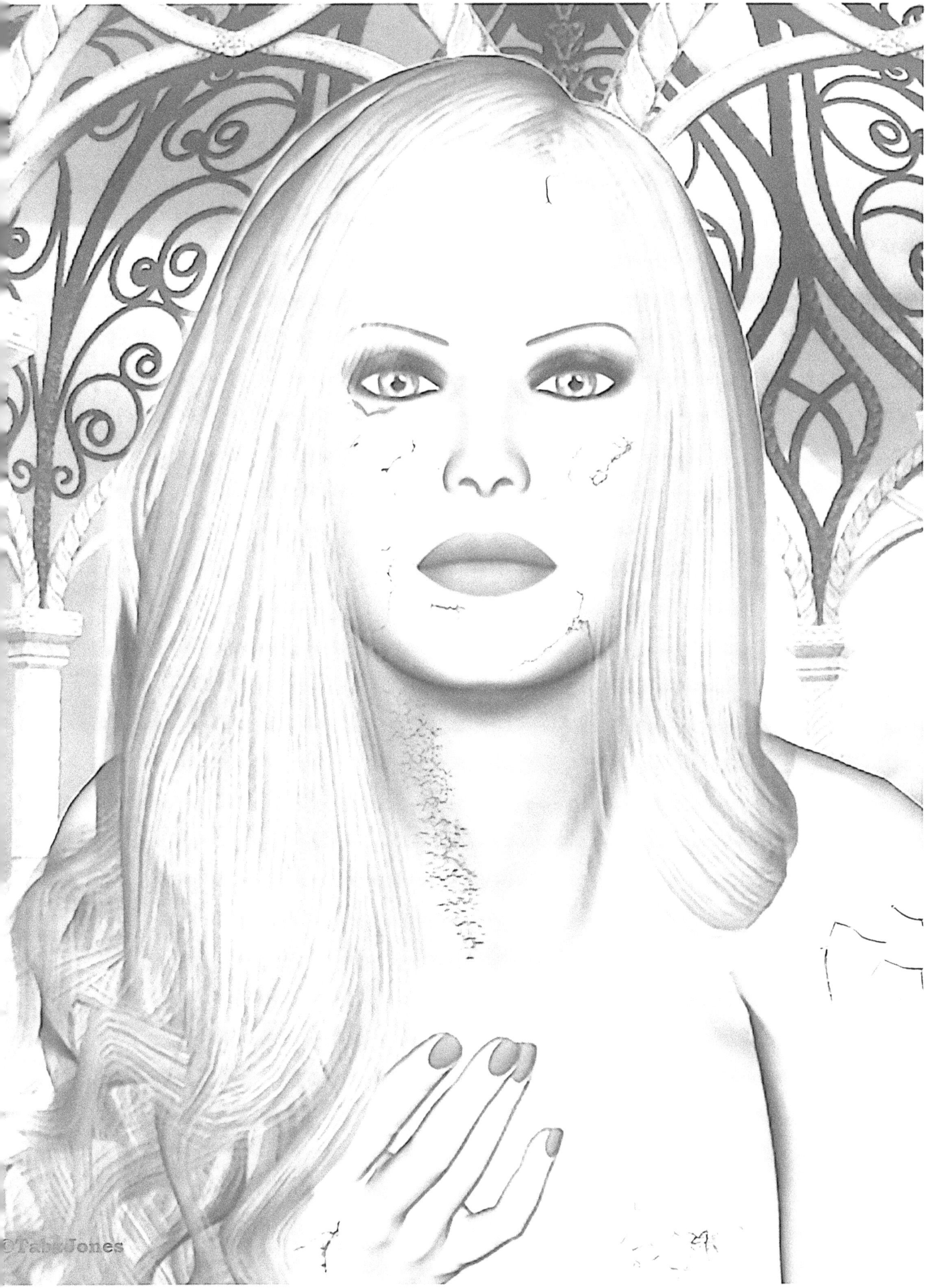
©TabzJones

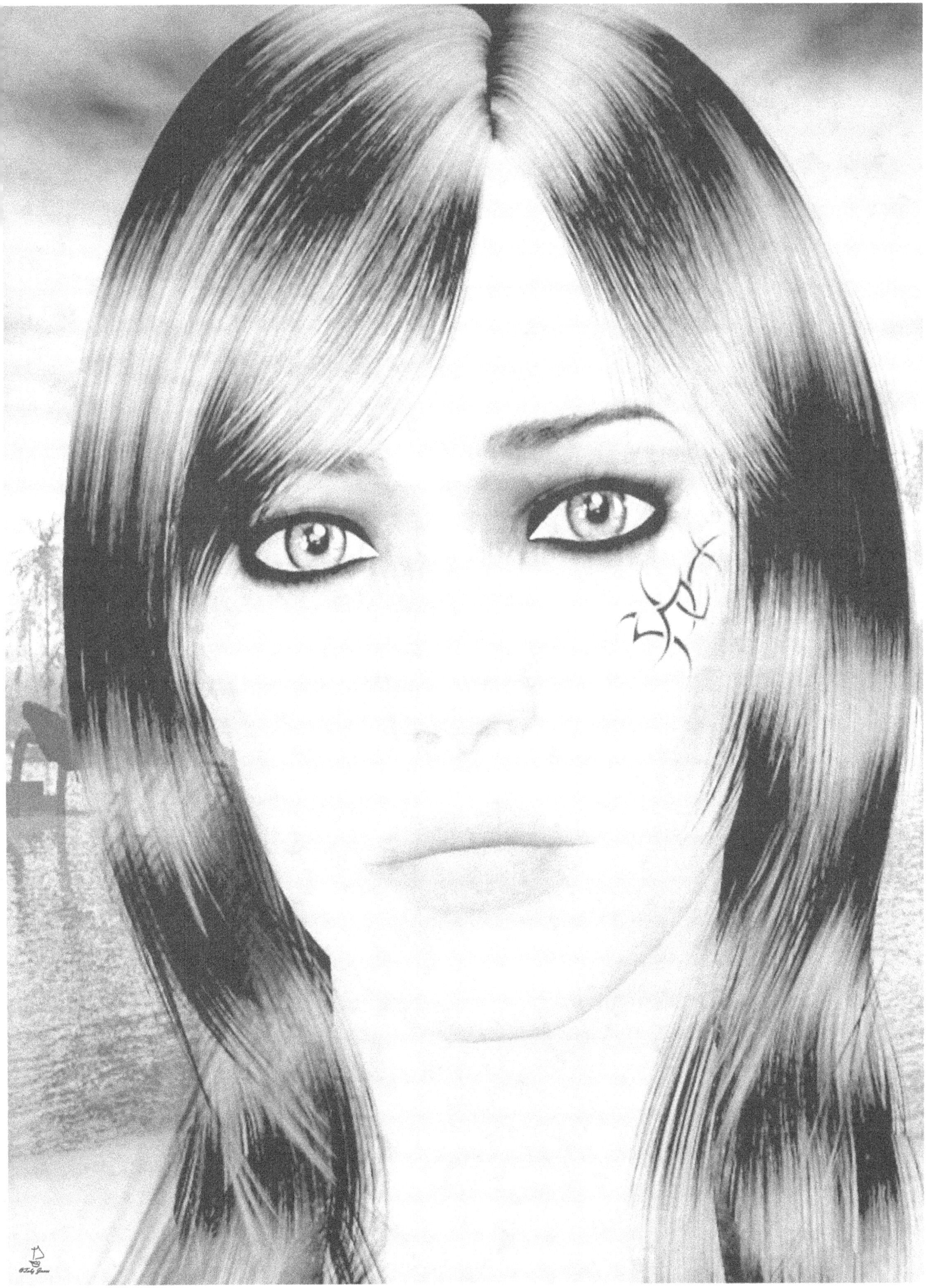

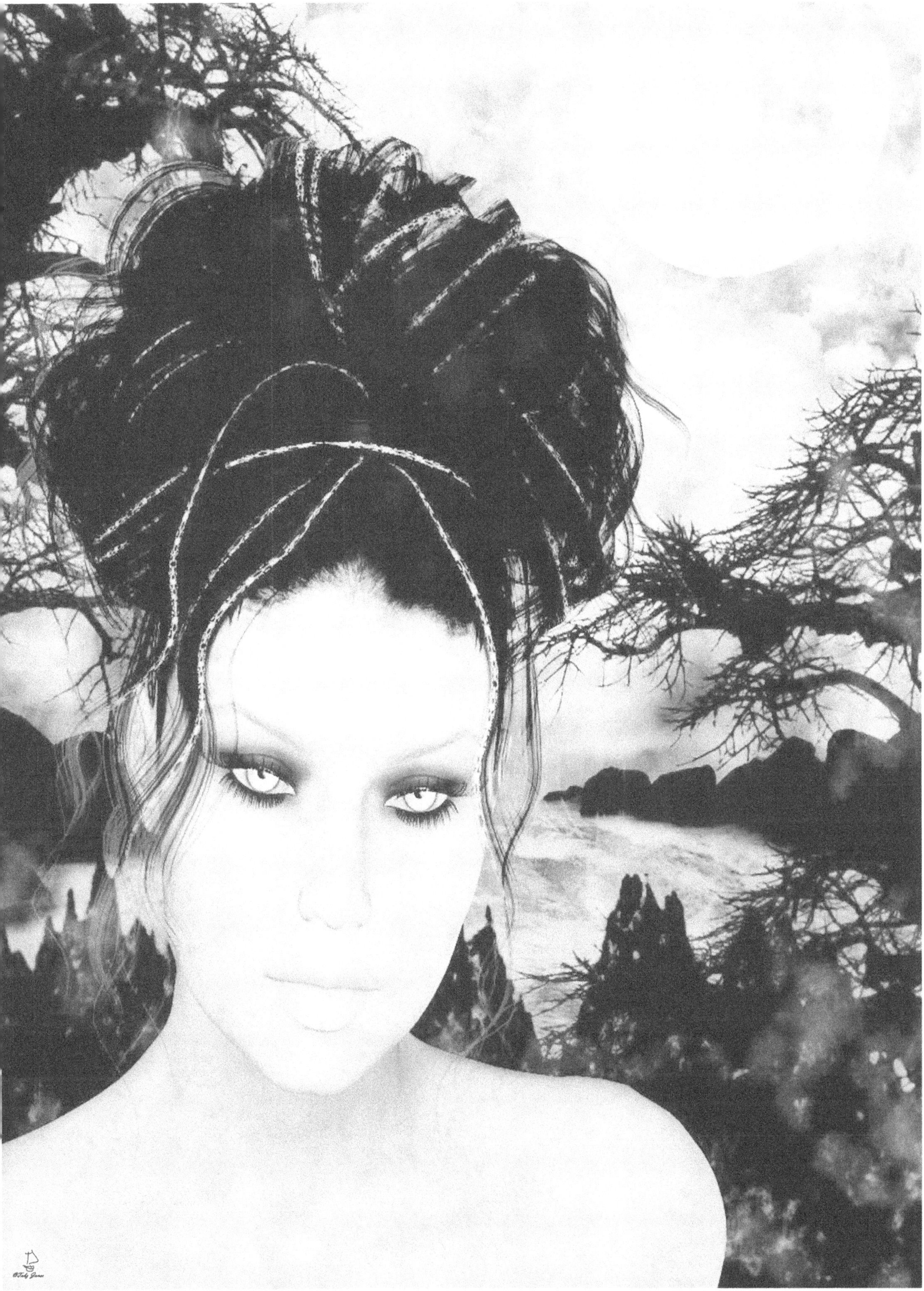

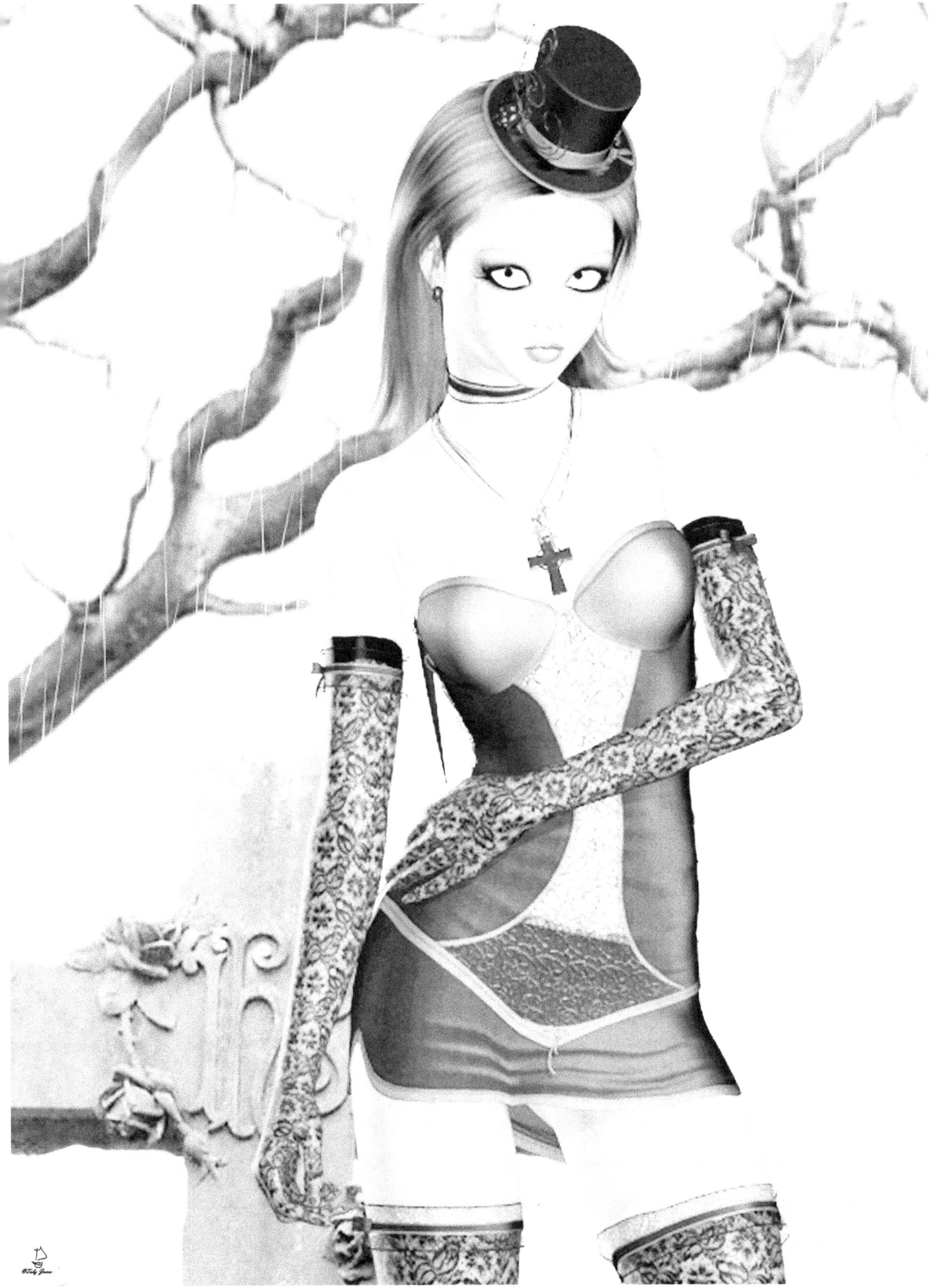

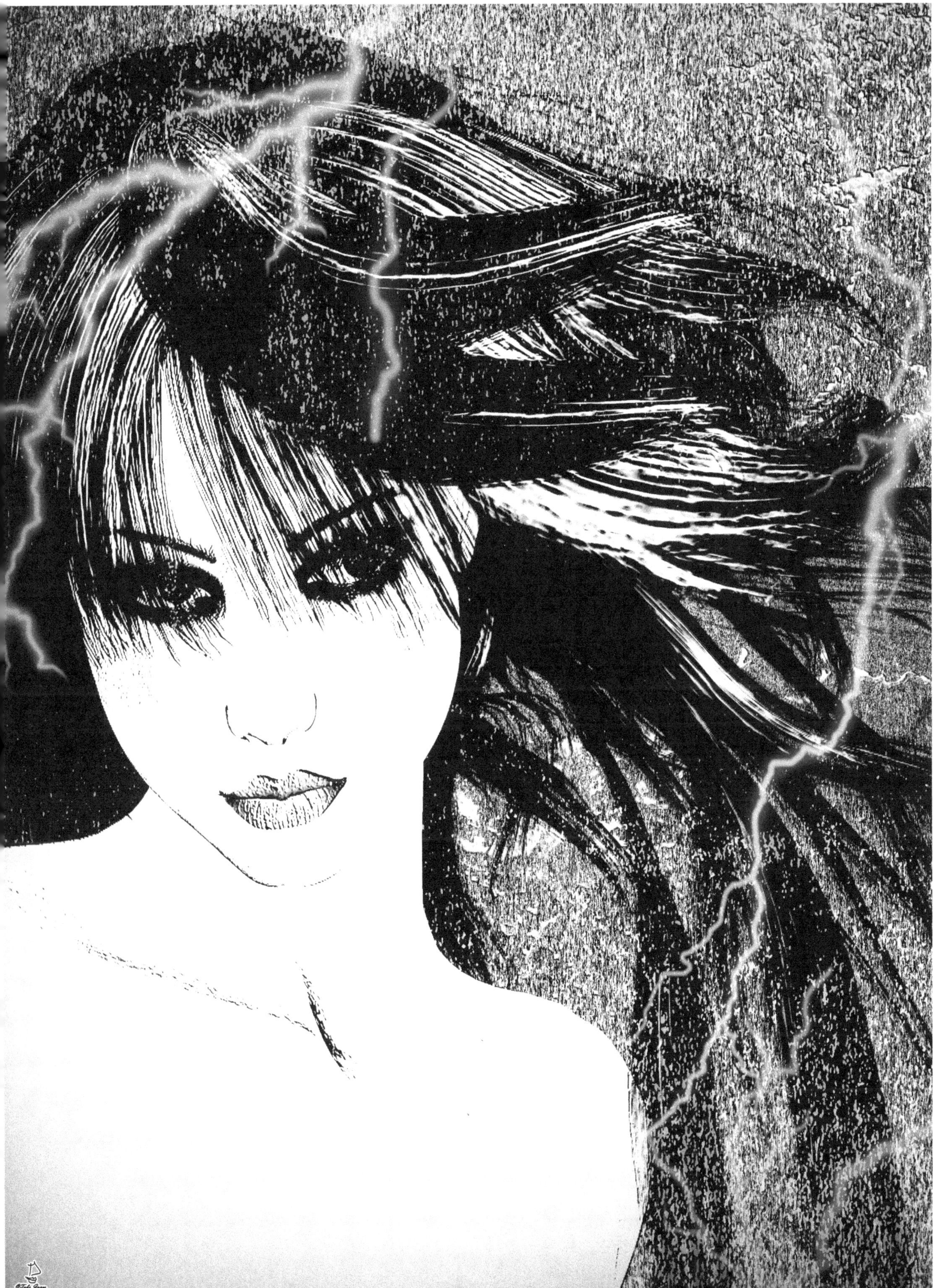

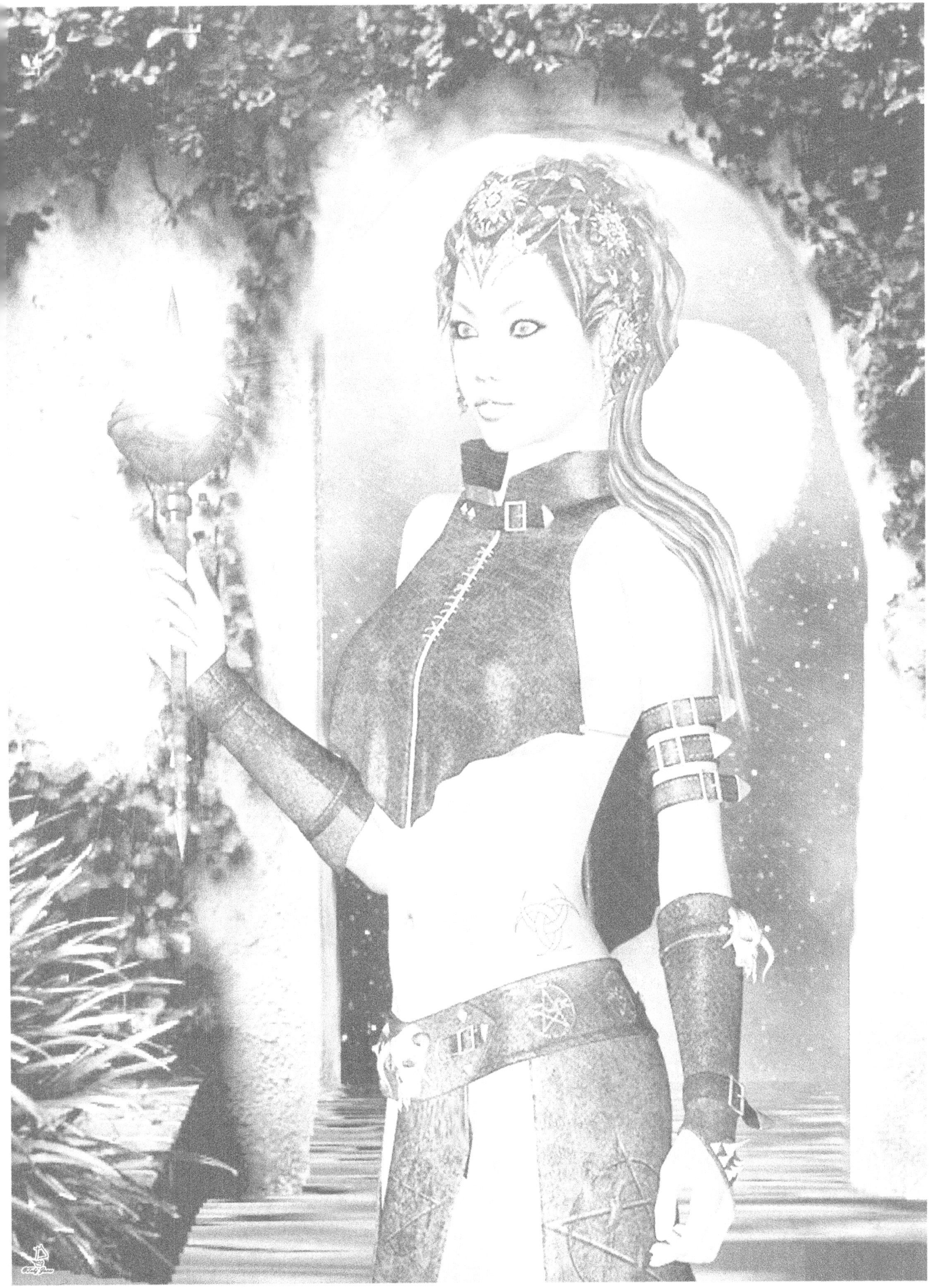

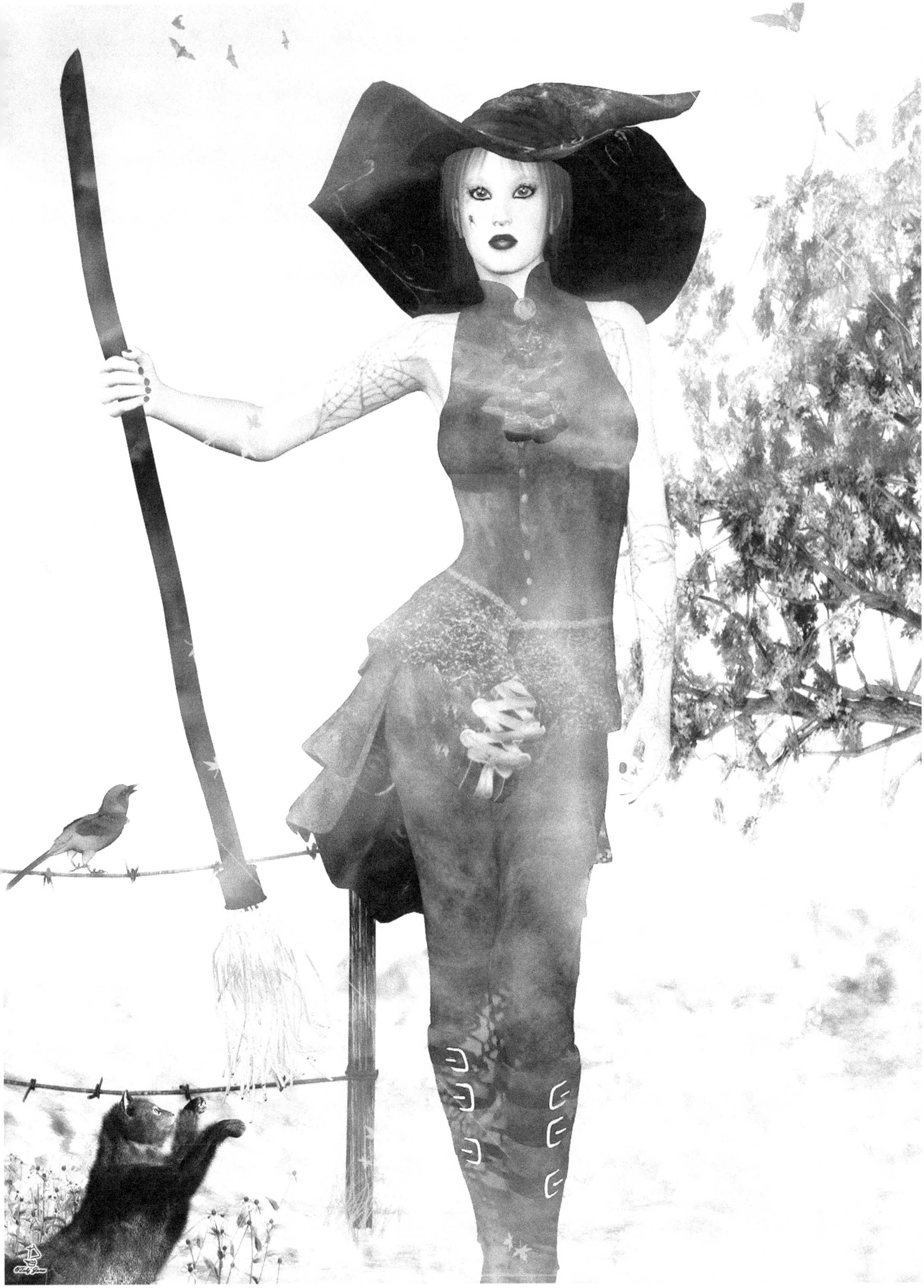

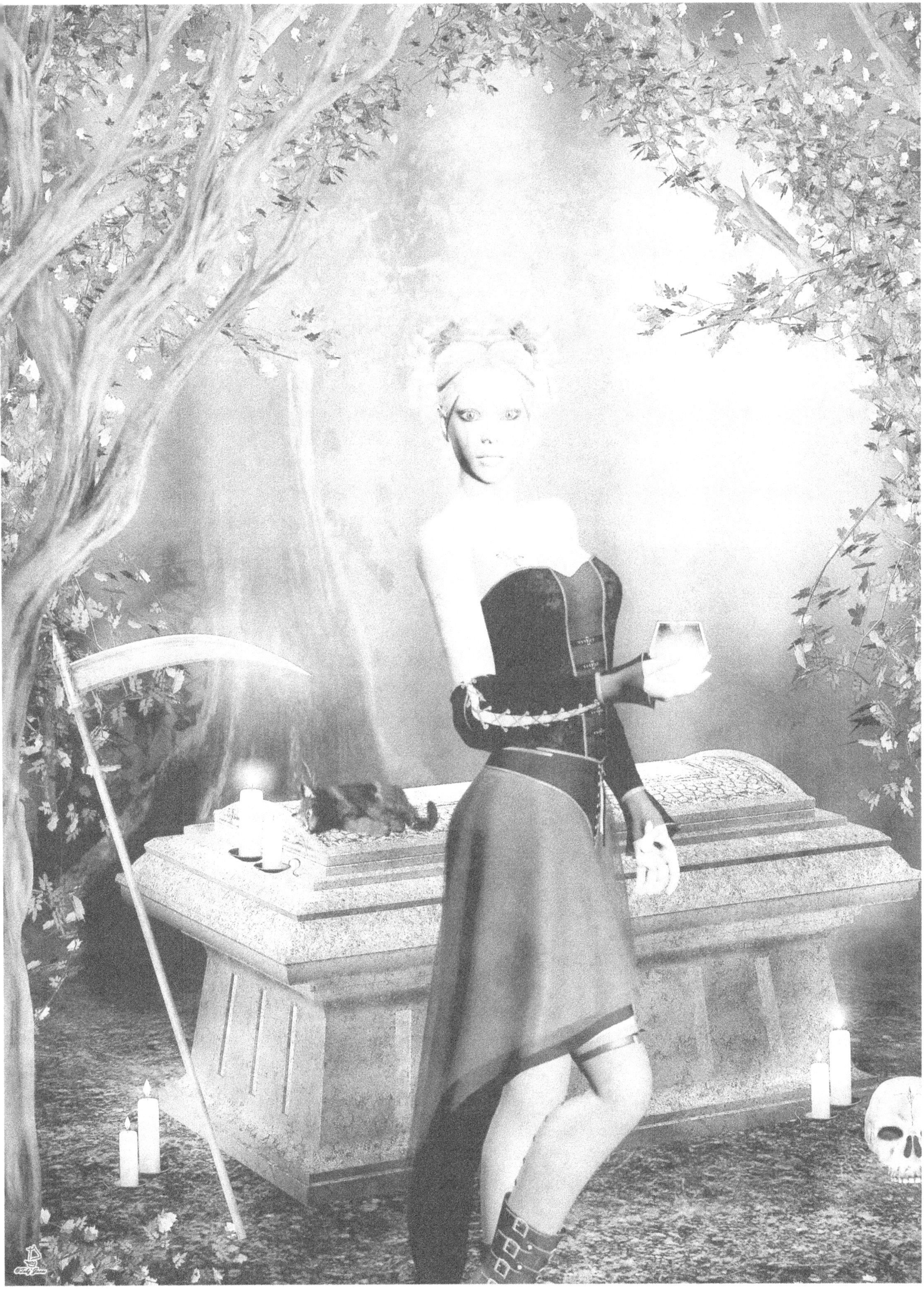

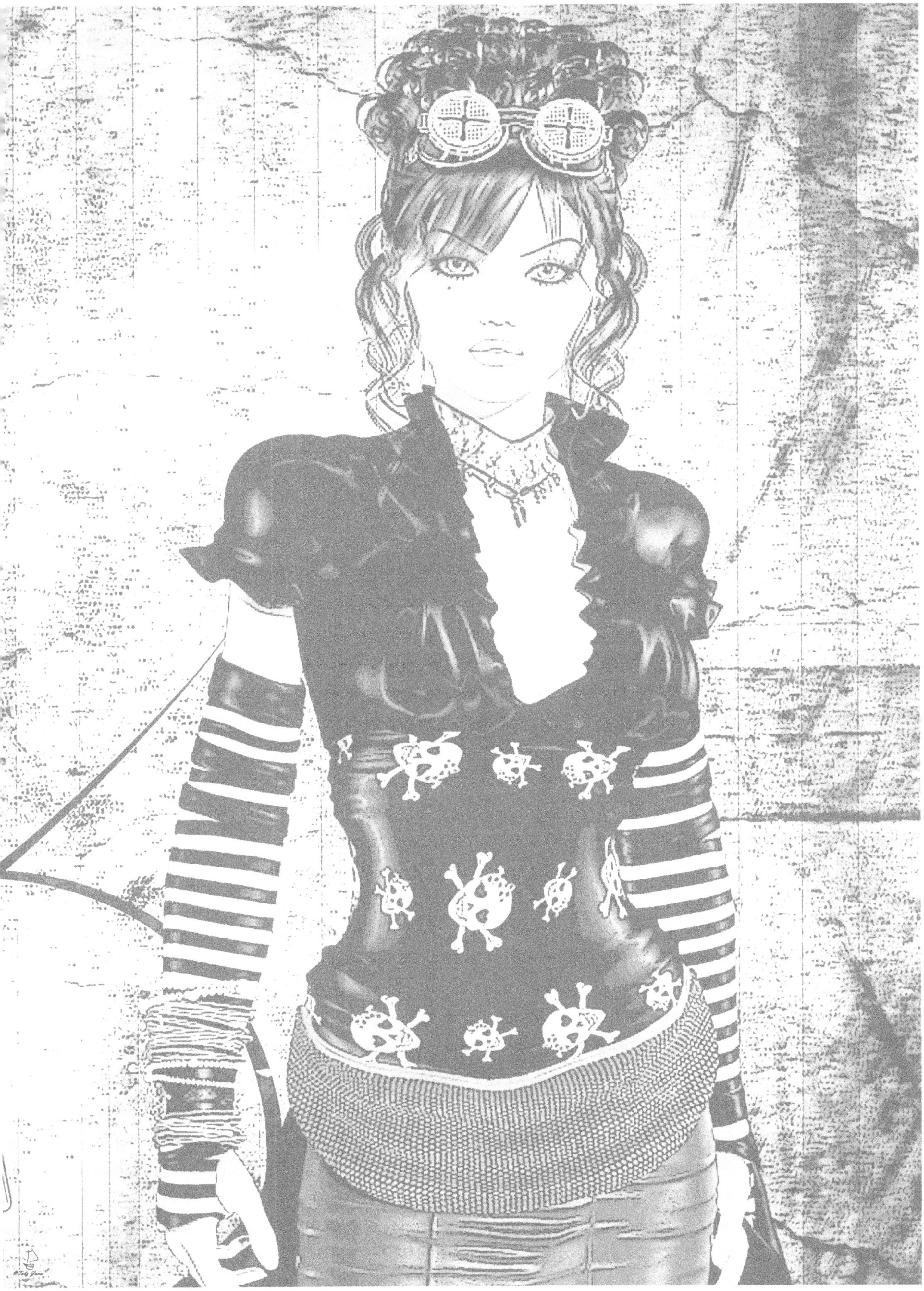

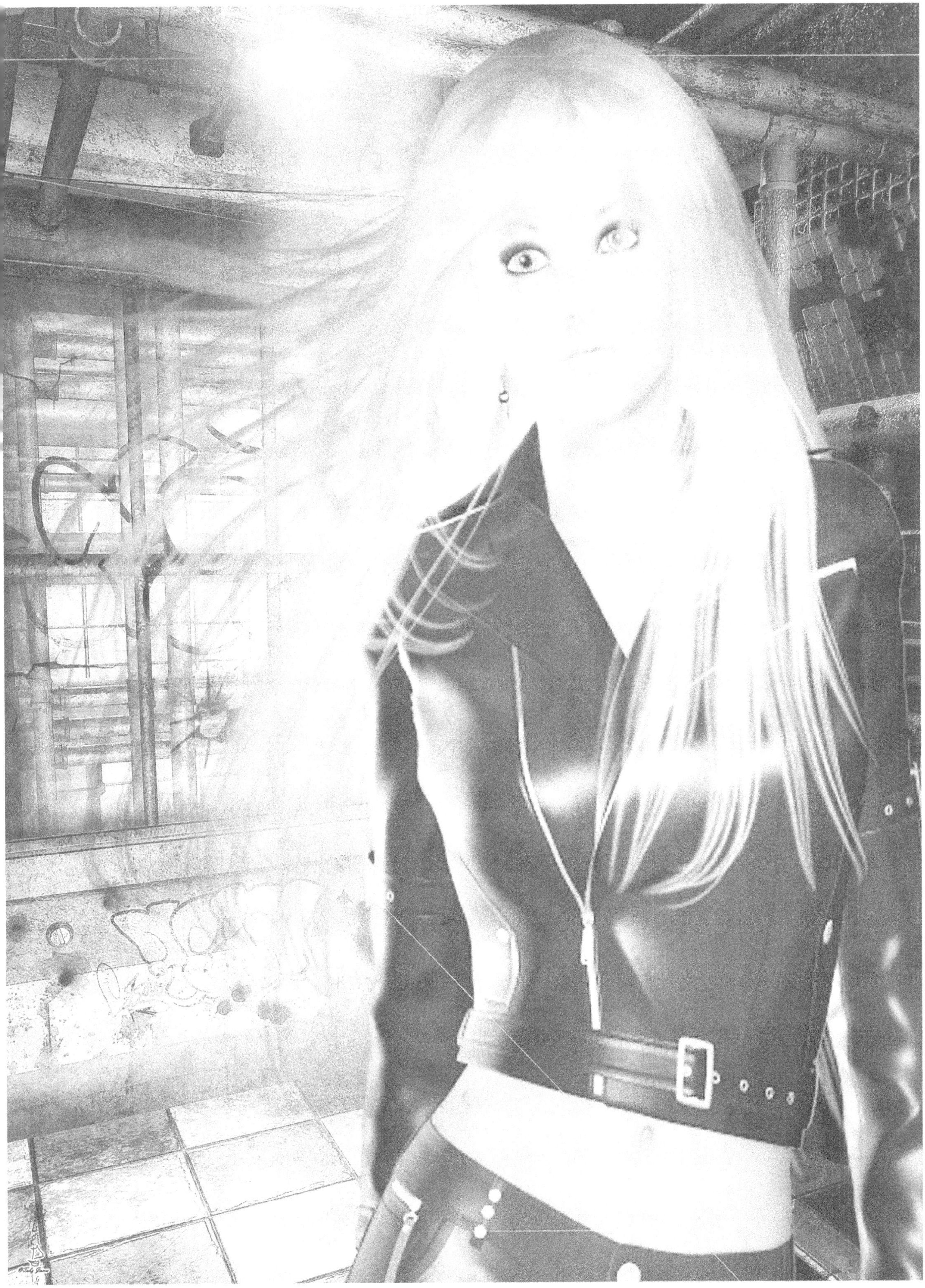

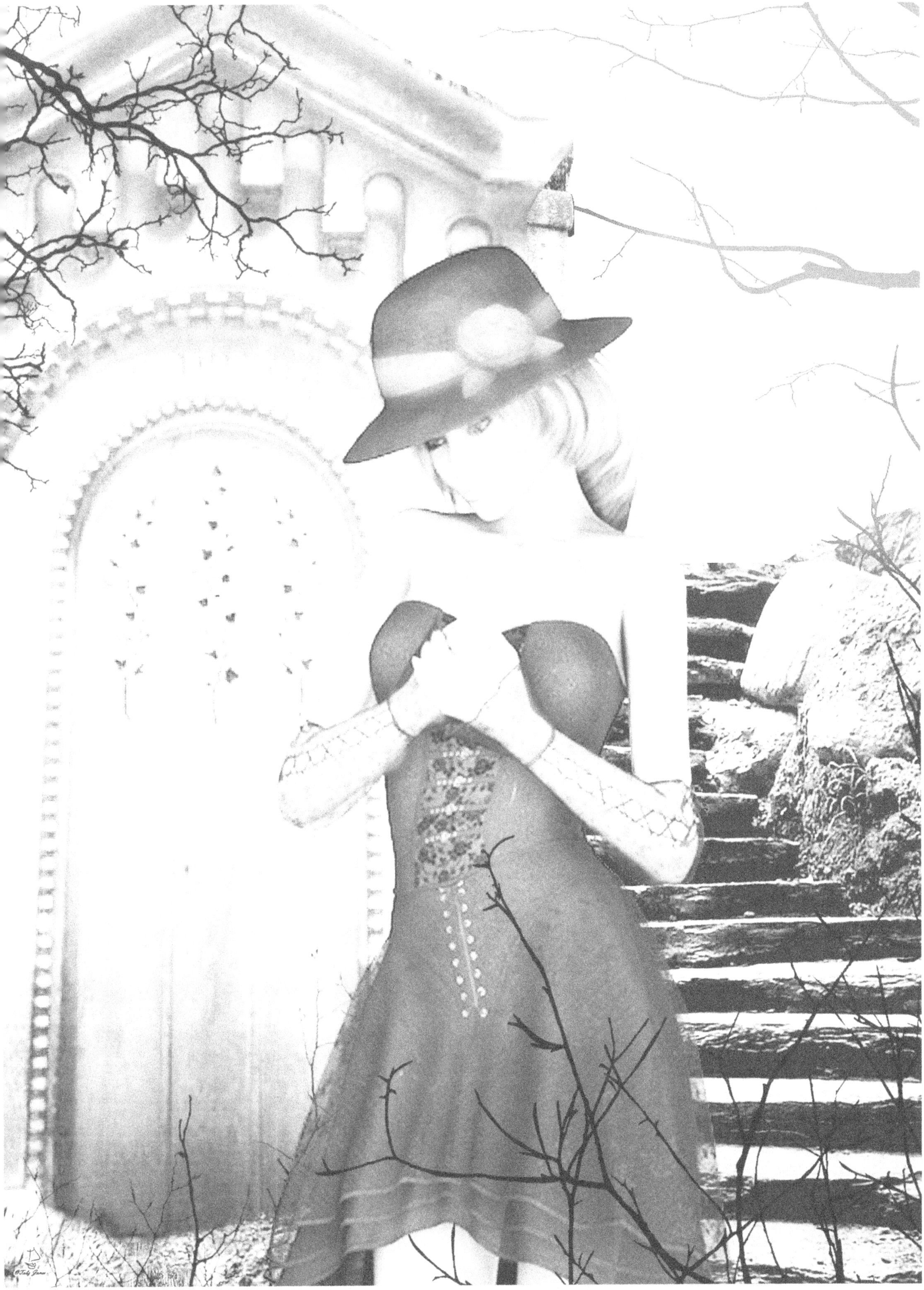

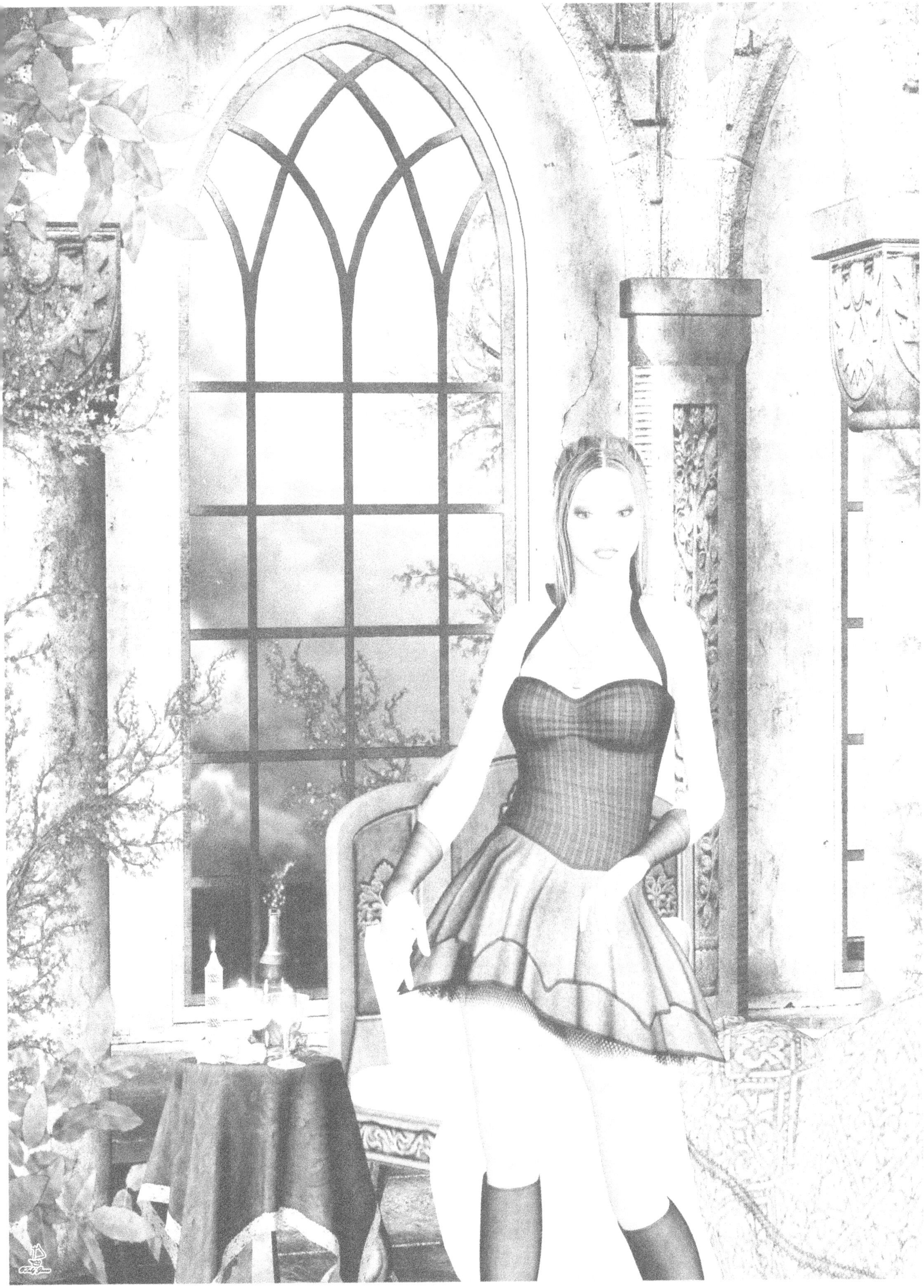

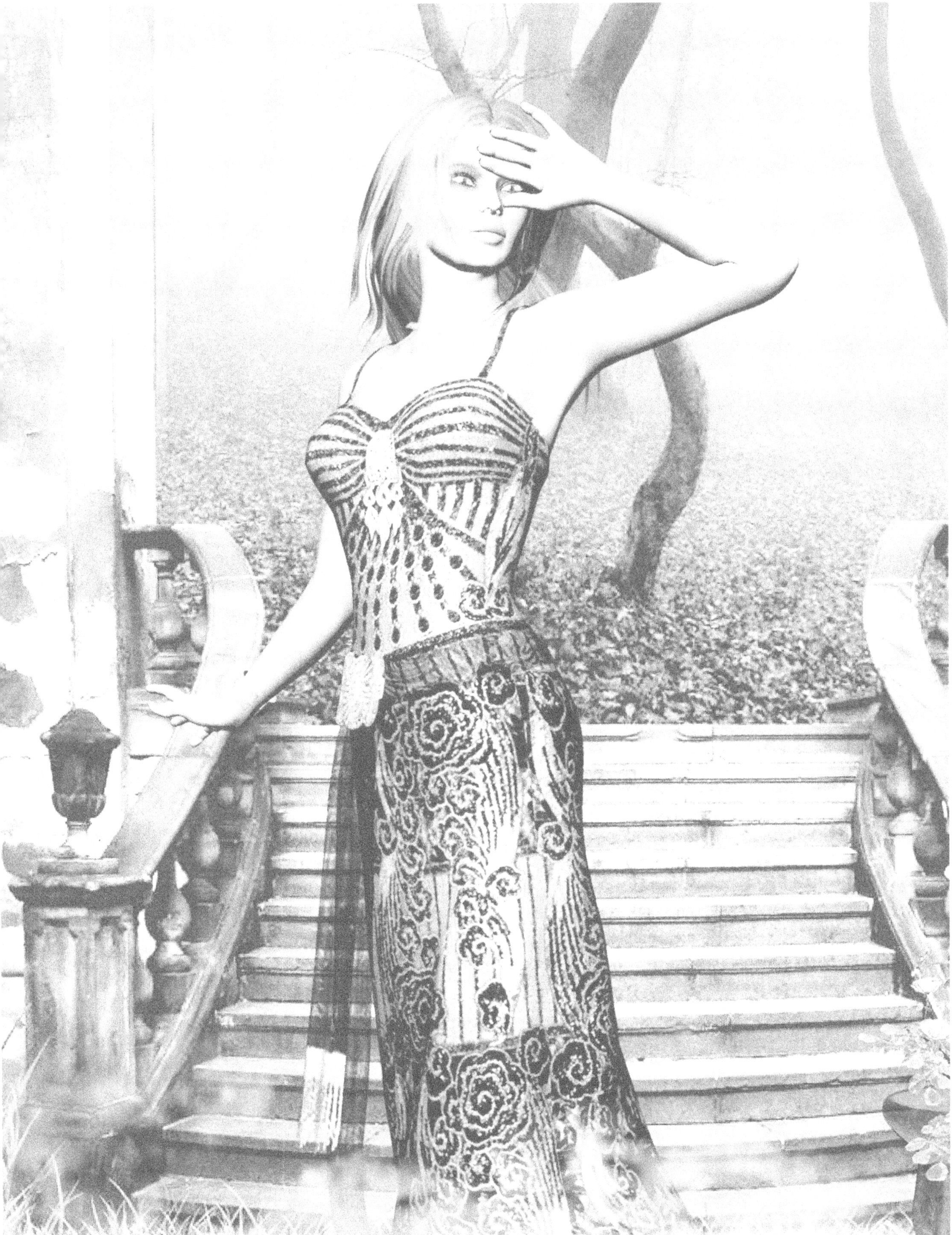

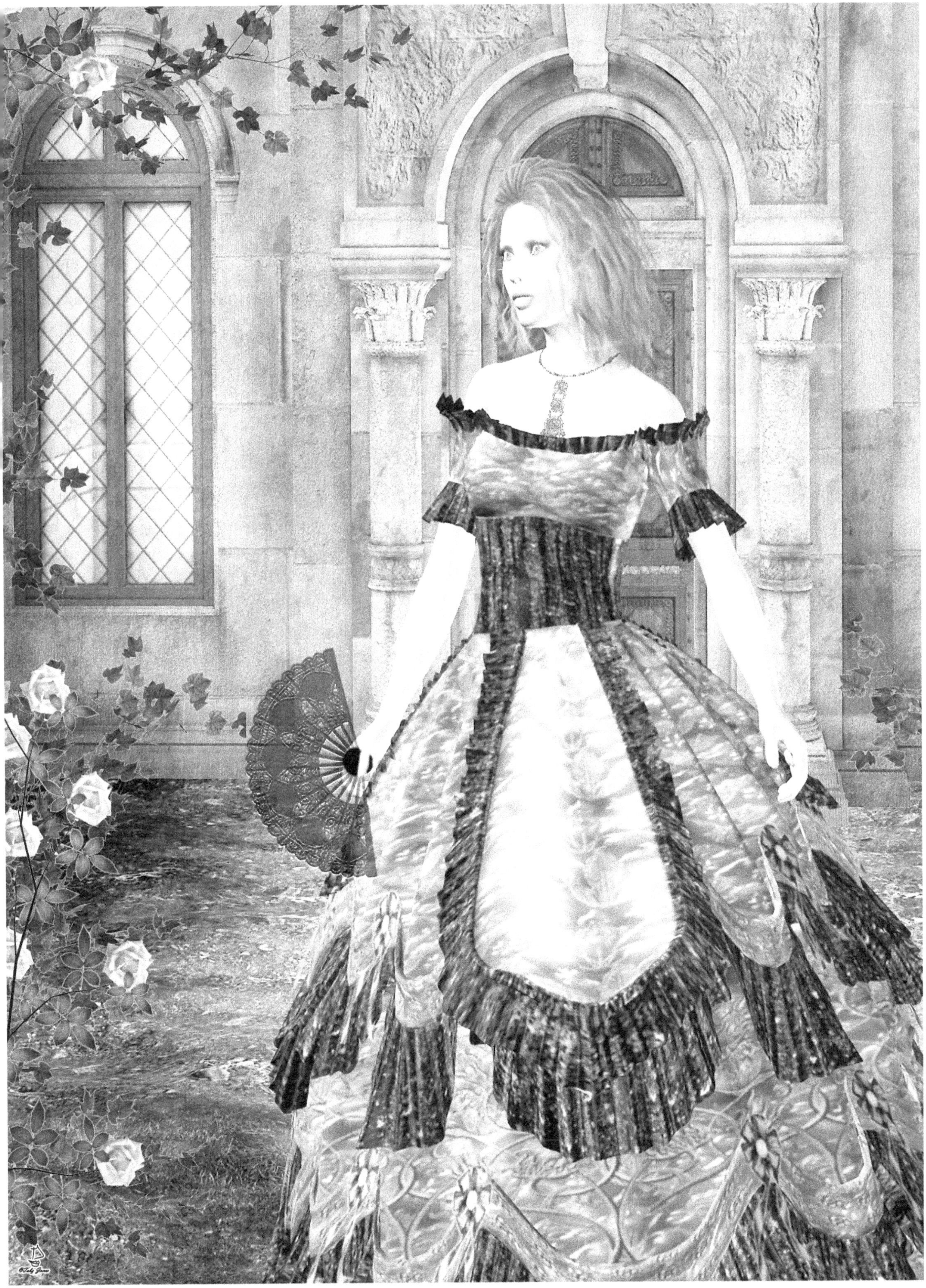

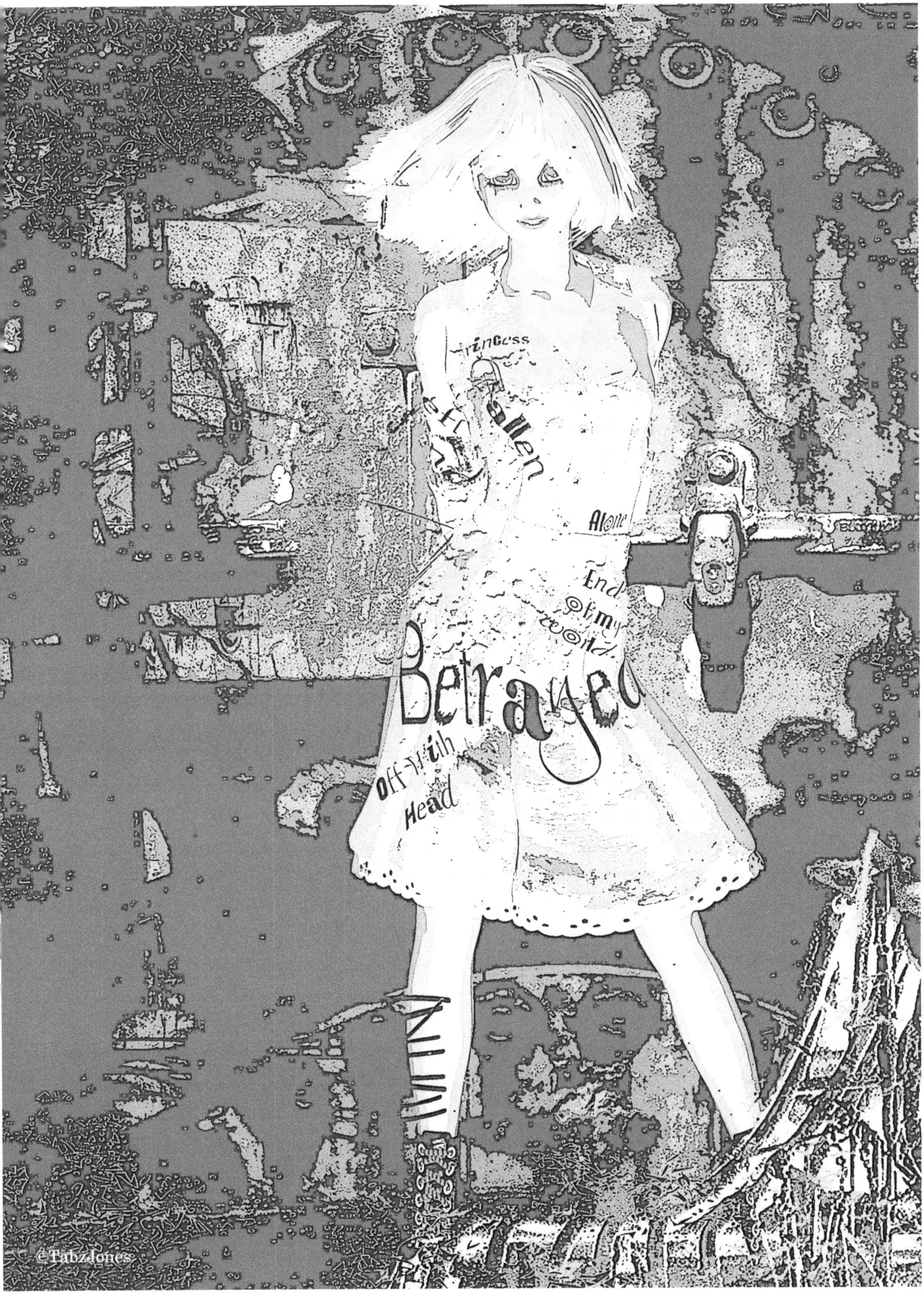

Princess
Fallen
Alone
End of my world
Betrayed
Off with Head
©TabzJones

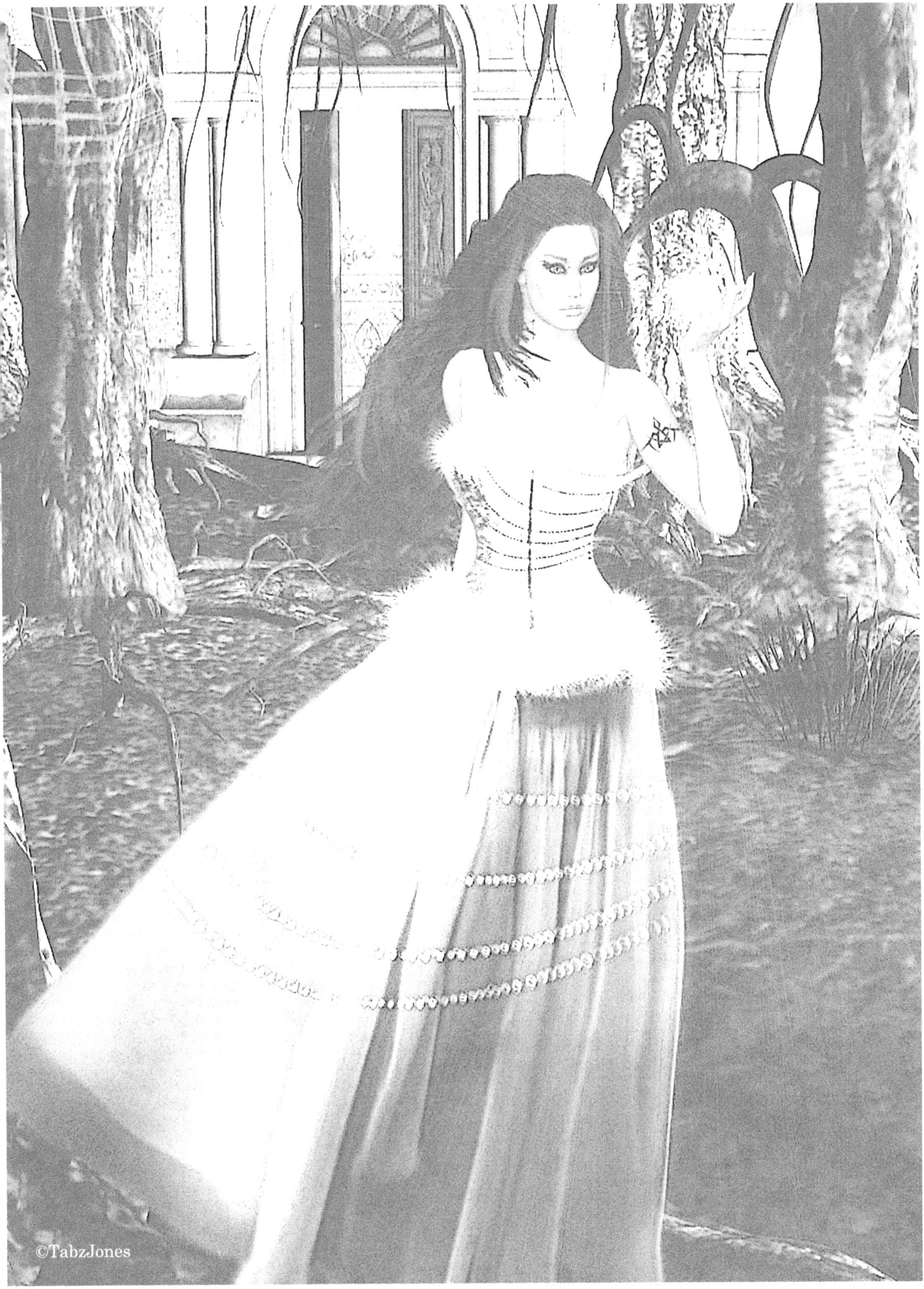
©TabzJones

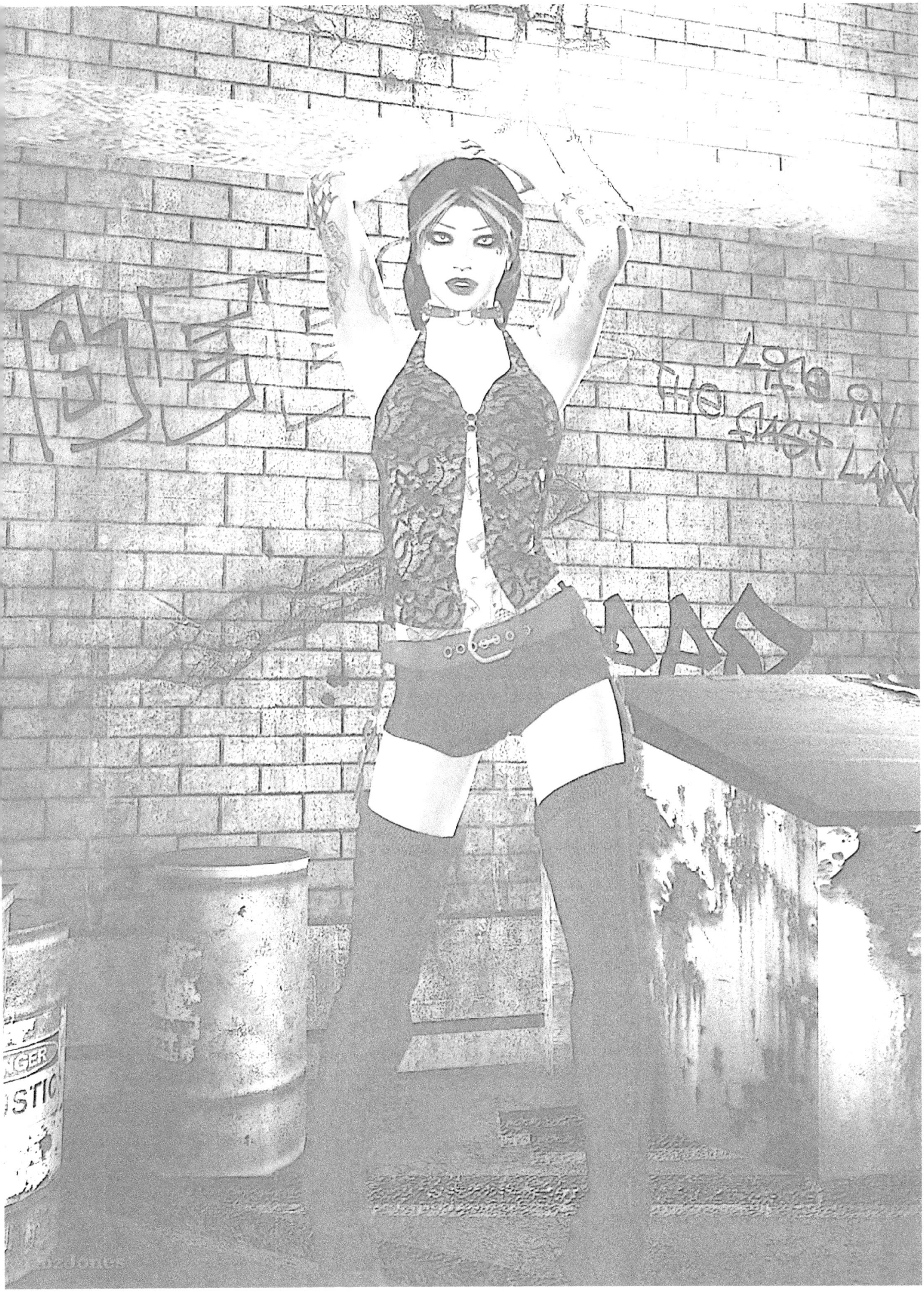

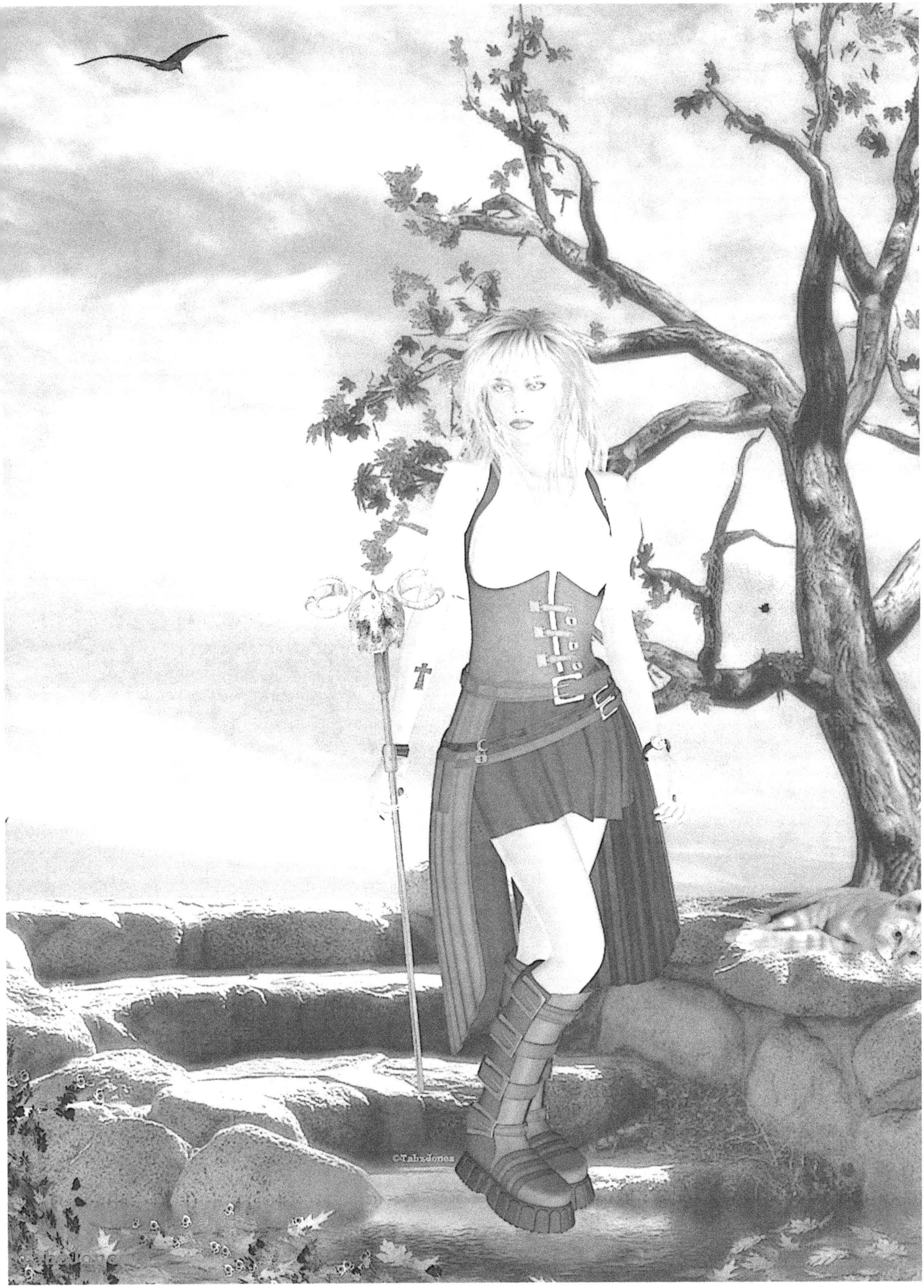
©TabzJones

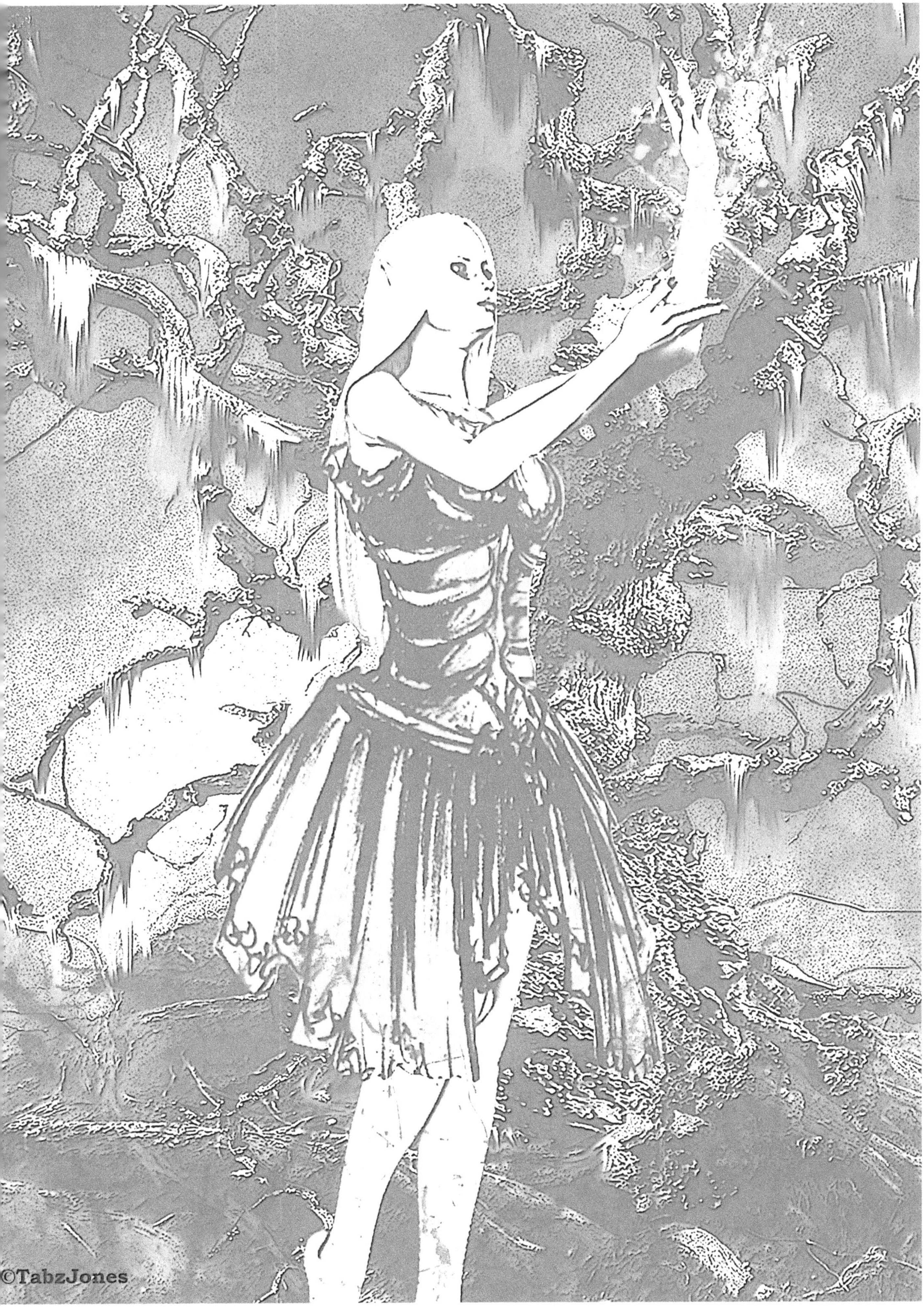
©TabzJones

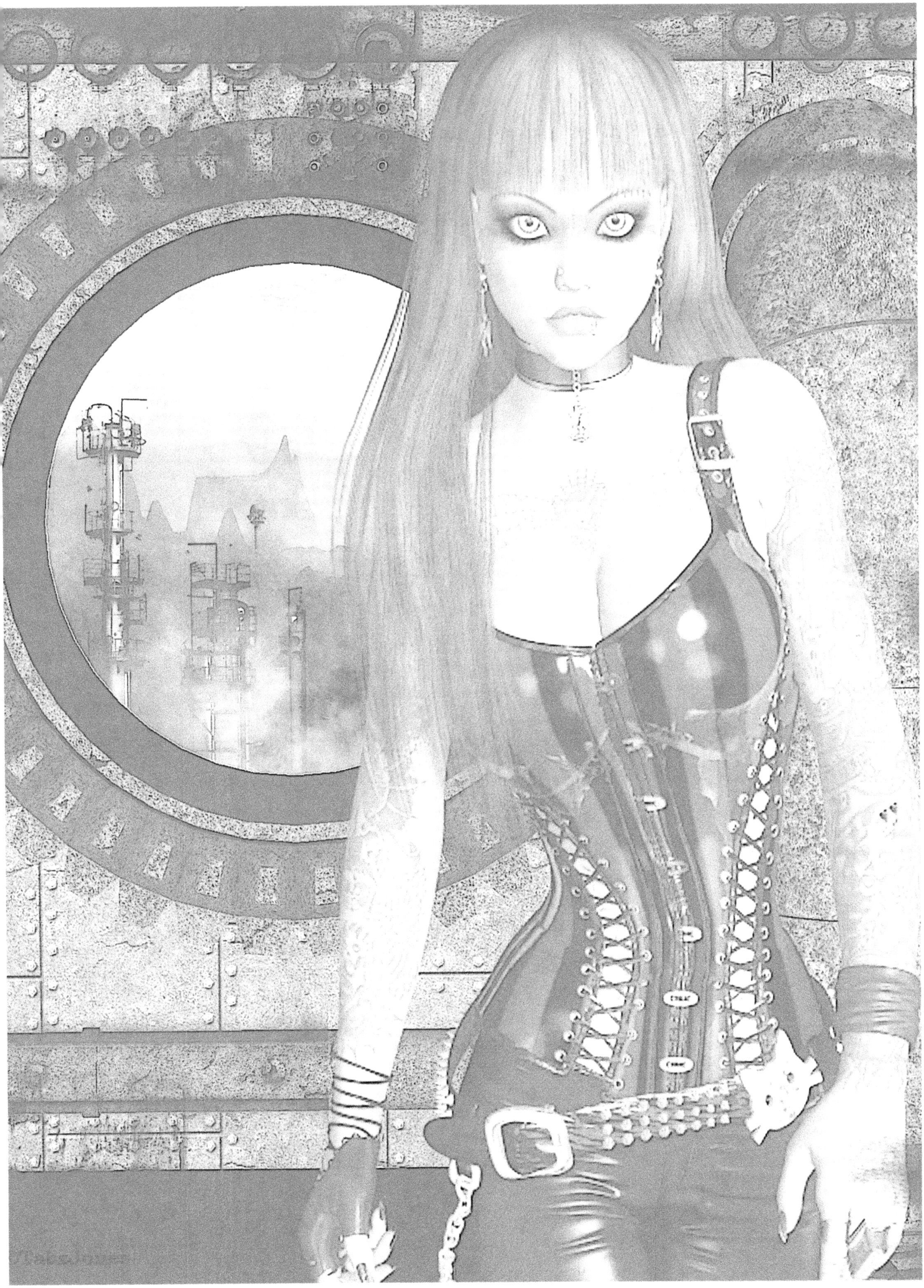

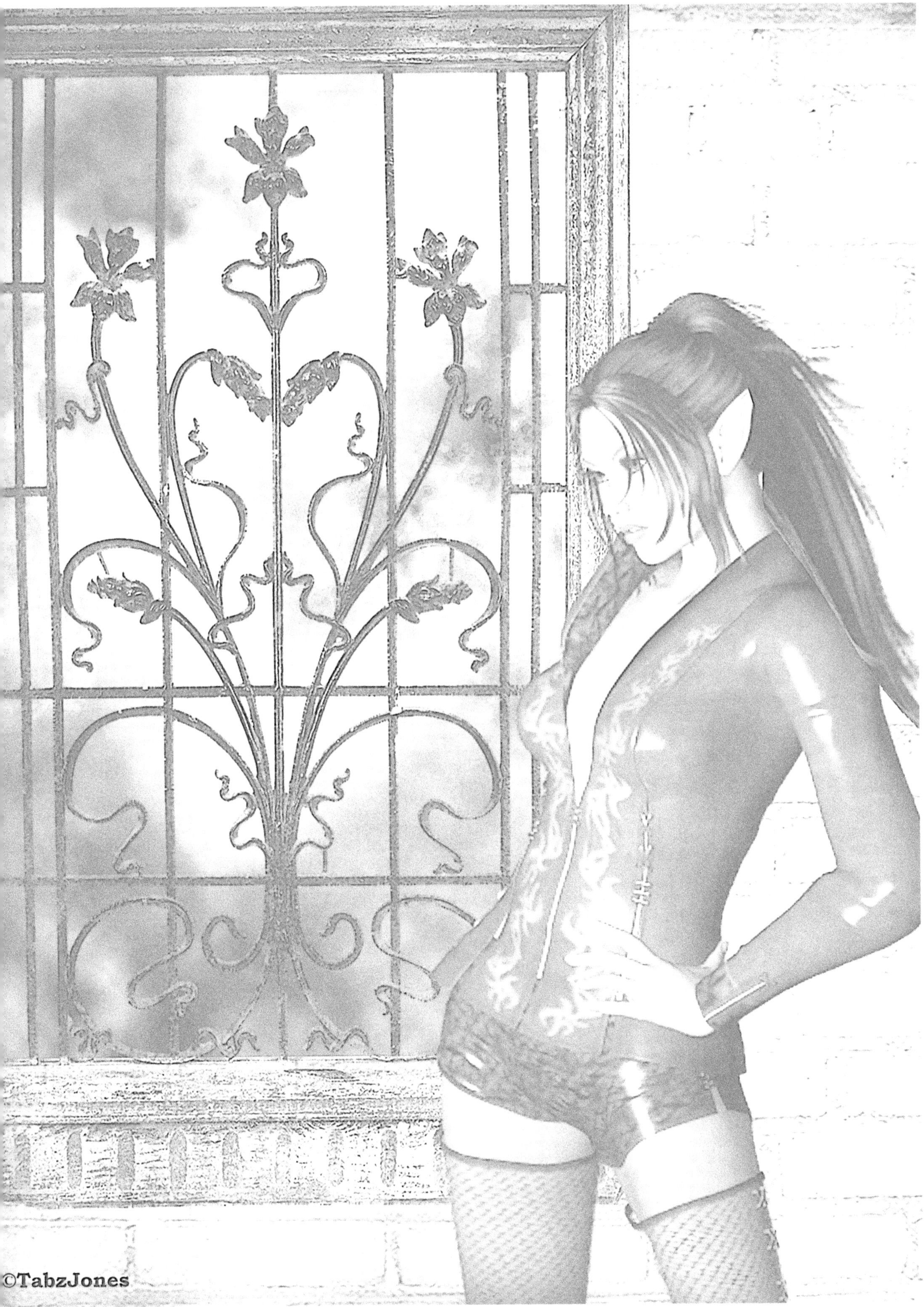
©TabzJones

www.ingramcontent.com/pod-product-compliance
Lightning Source LLC
Chambersburg PA
CBHW081257180526
45170CB00007B/2463
9781546307525